Holy Women of Great Perfection

Thirty Signs and Meanings of Ultimate Nature
in the Ancient Tibetan Tradition

Holy Women of Great Perfection

Thirty Signs and Meanings of Ultimate Nature in the Ancient Tibetan Tradition

From the *White Sky Primordial Mind-Essence Clearance of Extremes: Cycle of Essential Instructions of the Male and Female Lineages*

Commentary by
Geshe Dangsong Namgyal

Namkha Publications
Freedom, California

Copyright © 2021 Geshe Dangsong Namgyal

All Rights Reserved. No part of this book may be reproduced or transmitted in any form or by any means, electronic or mechanical, including photocopying, recording, or by any information storage and retrieval system, without permission in writing from the publisher.
ISBN: 978-0-9996898-2-0

Translation by Geshe Namgyal and David Molk
Traditional line drawings created by Norbu Lhundrub

Library of Congress Control Number: 2021942633

Namkha Publications
P.O. Box 65
Freedom CA 95019 USA
namkha2018@yahoo.com

https://www.kunsanggarcenter.org/namkha

Contents

Foreword vii
Holy Women of Great Perfection 1
Satrig Ersang 11
No. 1 Dakini Dzema Yiwongma 13
No. 2 Dakini Ulishag 17
No. 3 Dakini Namkha Ökyi Gyelmo 19
No. 4 Dakini Salwa Yingchug Ma 23
No. 5 Dakini Ökyi Lama 27
No. 6 Dakini Kharmokyong 31
No. 7 Dakini Mang-je Salgye-ö 37
No. 8 Dakini Dutsi-kyong 41
No. 9 Dakini Thuchen 45
No. 10 Dakini Selwa Ödrön 49
No. 11 Dakini Drimé Dangden Ma 53
No. 12 Dakini Ökyi Dzutrul Tön 57
No. 13 Dakini Dzutrul Natsog Tön 61
No. 14 Dakini Nangwa Datön Ma 65
No. 15 Dakini Tog-beb Ma 69
No. 16 Dakini Namkha Cham 71
No. 17 Dakini Ötang Ma 75
No. 18 Dakini Gyan-den Ma 77
No. 19 Dakini Drag-chen Tsal 81
No. 20 Dakini Namkha Nyima Öden Ma 85
No. 21 Dakini Nyima Tong-Kyab Ma 89
No. 22 Dakini Maha Sukasiddhi 93
No. 23 Dakini Bon-chig 95
No. 24 Dakini Bon-chig 97
No. 25 Dakini Bon-chig 99
No. 26 Dakini Bon-chig 101
No. 27 Dakini Bon-chig 105
No. 28 Dakini Bon-chig 111
No. 29 Dakini Bon-chig 115
No. 30 Dakini Bon-chig 119
Questions and Answers 121
The Root Text 133
Additional Meditation 146
About Geshe Namgyal 151
Acknowledgments 153

Dedication

This book is dedicated to all my kind, wise teachers in great appreciation of their tireless guidance. It is offered for the benefit and liberation of my students, and all sentient beings. May all negative energies in the world be pacified.

Foreword

In the scriptures of highest Buddhist Tantra of the ancient Bön tradition, the ultimate truth is revealed: that all beings have the same potential for full awakening and compassionate action, regardless of their gender orientation. What is further clarified is that the masculine and feminine principals are unified in a fully awakened state of being. In Buddha's assertion of the existence of buddha nature in all beings, we can find what is surely the deepest and purest message of all spirituality: the equality and essential goodness of all living beings.

This message of all the holy beings has been distorted over the course of time and concealed by human imperfection and patriarchal dominance. I am therefore especially gladdened to be bringing forth this new translation and commentary from our ancient Bön tradition of teachings given solely by enlightened women. They are from many countries: India, China, Pakistan, Iran, Kashmir, Nepal, Tibet, Zhangzhung. In the concise root text, each of the Dakinis gives a teaching in mystical sign language, followed by a verbal explanation that nakedly reveals the true nature of mind. It is a brief root text that is part of the *Yetri Thasel* cycle in the Dzogchen teachings of Bön.

In my lifetime of study and practice, I have personally found the practice of these teachings to be the most beneficial. I have also found it to be a most useful meditation to offer to others. With prayers and aspirations that it may bring temporary and ultimate benefit to a wide readership, I invite you to enjoy this new translation of the root text and the commentary that I have prepared with translation and editing assistance of David Molk.

—*Geshe Dangsong Namgyal, California, July 2021*

Satrig Ersang, the Great Mother

Holy Women of Great Perfection

Thirty Signs and Meanings of Ultimate Nature in the Ancient Tibetan Tradition

From the *White Sky Primordial Mind-Essence Clearance of Extremes: Cycle of Essential Instructions of the Male and Female Lineages*

The root text is part of the great general Tantra "*White Space Liberating Extremes of the Mind.*" In that text, we will now focus on the Guru Yoga that is part of the *Dakini Lineage of Pure Dzogchen*. This is a blessed lineage, a post-visionary lineage. An extensive explanation of this subject would require quite a lot of study of the Sutra, Tantra and philosophical systems in an extremely profound and comprehensive way. In order to give a full understanding of these teachings, an explanation given in the monastery would go into great detail. In this teaching, however, we will not delve into such a full study of the subject.

What is presented to you herein is the essence of the teaching in a way that you can understand and be able to bring to fruition. As you practice, you will be able to comprehend it more and more, just like the sun rising and gradually illuminating the world. This will depend upon your conviction, faith, and the degree to which you aspire. This is not saying that faith is sufficient; it does require investigation and looking at the logic behind it. Study, practice and experience must come together. The object is to actually attain insight into reality and to see how things truly exist. But faith in dharma, and faith in the value of the Natural Mind, are the essential and principal factors. Based on reliance and conviction, we can develop a deeper and more profound understanding, and eventually gain realization. That is why Guru Yoga is important.

Guru Yoga

For this Guru Yoga, we will visualize the image of *Satrig Ersang*, the Great Mother, the Loving Goddess of Wisdom. Visualize her in the space before you at whatever size is comfortable. The many *Dakinis* or enlightened women who are in this lineage are all emanations of the Great Mother. Visualize her body, not as ordinary and not like a two-dimensional drawing or painting, but as a light body in the nature of compassion and transcendent wisdom. Understand the immense significance of the Great Mother; she is the basis or foundation of all the Buddhas. All of the Buddhas arise and manifest from her as emanation bodies and complete enjoyment bodies, nirmanakayas and sambhogakayas. All Buddha emanations arise from her.

Sit in your usual meditation posture. Visualize that from the heart of the Great Mother, Satrig Ersang, rainbow colored light emanates in the nature of fire. It comes to you, strikes you, fills you with light and burns away all of your ignorance, afflicted and deluded states of mind, and all hindrances or obscurations to understanding the true nature of existence. This is a wisdom fire that first burns away all ignorance and obscurations.

Secondly, visualize light emanating from her heart entering

into you in the form of wisdom water and cleansing away all negativities and obscurations.

Thirdly, visualize light emanating from her heart in the nature of wisdom wind which, when it strikes you, blows away all conceptual thoughts, delusions, and samsara.

Visualize that from the crown of the Great Mother a white *AH* (ཨ) syllable, of the nature of the transcendent wisdom of the Buddha, comes forth and dissolves into your own crown. Feel that from this *AH* entering and dissolving into your crown, you receive all of the physical attributes and qualities of an enlightened body. Then visualize that from the Great Mother's throat, a red *OM* (ཨོཾ) syllable emanates forth and dissolves into your own throat, and that you receive all of the qualities of enlightened speech. Then visualize that from the heart of the Great Mother, a blue *HUNG* (ཧཱུྃ) emanates forth and dissolves into your own heart, and that through this you receive all the qualities of the enlightened mind. Feel that all obstacles and resistance to understanding the teachings are cleared away and that you have become a perfect receptacle, a perfect vessel to receive these instructions. Understand and rejoice in that!

This meditation serves as the empowerment or initiation. Feel that you have now received the power to understand what Tibetans call the *neluk* (*gnas lugs*), the true nature of the mind. Here we speak of it as being Natural Mind. The blessing that we receive in this empowerment is the capacity to understand and to realize the Natural Mind. It is also compared to awakening. Whereas ignorance or unknowing is like sleep, this is awakening into an illumination of understanding. It is a matter of decisive determination, free of hope and fear. In this state, we have already fallen off the top of the mountain. There is nothing else to look for or expect. It is sweet, like molasses or brown sugar, in that you understand all phenomena to be of a single taste in the Natural Mind. You see all phenomena, all forms, sounds and so on, of whatever size or color, as being like the waves of the ocean. They may be large or small, but they are all of the same nature as the ocean.

You also see all phenomena as similar to the sky or space. We have all kinds of pleasant and painful experiences, but with realization they cannot affect us; they are like space, like clarity. When these feelings and experiences arise, it is the result of the Guru Yoga rising within us and is what is called receiving the initiation or empowerment. This kind of experience arises through the practice of Guru Yoga, which is to be practiced continuously day to day. It can benefit in clearing away daily problems or difficulties that are encountered. But even more benefits can manifest in the future, at the time of death and beyond.

We can now receive the empowerment of the Great Mother, Sartrig Ersang, the basis for the emanation of all the Buddhas. We can also recognize her as the principal Buddha, the main Buddha of all. Compared to Christian and other religions, she would be God. In many religions, God tends to be seen in a male aspect but in this ancient tradition, she was seen as mother. That was our attitude in ancient Tibet, that the deity was a woman. I see that as natural. It is she that we visualize as the very source of the Dzogchen teachings, and also the perfections or paramitas. She's the *Great Mother Perfection of Wisdom, Prajnaparamita*. She is also regarded as space, in the sense of space meaning selflessness or emptiness. Homage is paid to her as the source of all things, that in which all things abide and in which all things dissolve.

When you settle in meditative equipoise, it is this visualization upon which you focus. Likewise, when you arise as the deity, you see yourself in this aspect. The single sphere of reality, the single bindu, drop of reality of Natural Mind, is also her, the Great Mother. We each have this Great Mother within us, intrinsic to ourselves. It is always there; we are never separated from the Great Mother. She is not just as depicted in a scroll painting or thangka. She is rather the inseparability of emptiness and luminosity, of selflessness and clarity, which illuminates everything. Visualize the Great Mother in this way, in this outfit, colorful and with the ornaments and so on, in order to practice the Guru Yoga with her.

This scripture is spoken by the Great Mother. It comes to us through a succession or lineage of enlightened women. These Dakinis, or *Khandro* as we say in Tibetan, or enlightened women, are from all over Asia, from different places. The main subject of this scripture and commentary is the single sphere of the Natural Mind. If you have no experience with any Dzogchen teachings before, this may be rather difficult to approach, but familiarize yourself with further study and practice.

These teachings are focused on ultimate reality, selflessness, and special emptiness. At first, it can be difficult to integrate or comprehend these teachings. The emptiness we are describing here is in connection with your mind. It is within the context of everything that we experience in our environment; the relationship between the subject and object in our perception of forms, sounds, smells, tastes, and tangible objects. We need to understand our mind and how to hold our mind. Identifying and recognizing the mind is like catching a thief on an abandoned path. If you know that a thief is going to be coming along a particular path, you could wait there to capture that person. Identifying and recognizing the mind is like that. Another metaphor is that it is like someone trying to catch an animal. When the animal is attentive, you won't have much of a chance to catch it. It is only when they are slightly distracted that you can catch them. It is like this that we need to glimpse, identify or recognize the Natural Mind.

It is not sufficient to talk about it, describe it, or explain it; rather it has to be identified in your own experience. Once you identify it in your experience, "that is emptiness, that is the clarity," then you can really go on to discuss it, to explain it—once you have recognized these things in your own experience.

How do we introduce Natural Mind? We say that it is like a dream. When you are dreaming, it is as if everything is really happening, but in fact it is not. It is not real. Like that, our experiences are mental constructions. These fabrications of the mind are empty. They are like illusions. That is how we identify it. In Tibetan we call it *tongpa nyid* (*stong pa nyid*), emptiness, or in Sanskrit, *shunyata*. Mental fabrications are also like clouds in the sky, which gather and form, then dissipate and disappear. This emptiness is not ordinary vacuity. Rather, it is something that is self-arising and self-knowing and it is that from which all phenomena arise and dissolve.

It is with this understanding that you will realize the Great Mother. It is also what we call Bodhichitta in Sanskrit, or enlightenment mind. The Tibetan term is *jangchub sem* (*byang chub sems*). Each of these syllables has its own significance.

The first syllable, *jang*, is often translated as enlightenment, but literally means pure and expanded. It pertains to that which is primordially pure, having never been defiled or contaminated. It is the same for all living beings, human beings, animals, Buddhas—from the beginning; the Natural Mind is never defiled.

The second syllable, *chub*, means endowed with all of the qualities of the Buddha which are spontaneously present. There is no way of accomplishing or attaining Buddhahood or awakening that is not already included within it. All the sixty perfections are included. All of compassion is present in it, just like the sun, like space, like the ground, like the earth, like the river that is flowing continuously, never ceasing, never interrupted. It is a compassion that is impartial to all, just like the sun that shines on everything. It is like the earth in that no matter how much you use it, it is never used up. It is like space, in being something that we cannot understand with ordinary conceptual thought. All of these qualities are spontaneously present in Natural Mind. That is the meaning of the second syllable, *chub*.

The third syllable *sem*, which represents mind, means that the two qualities of "primordial purity" and "spontaneous presence" are inseparable. When we say mind in this context, it is not ordinary mind that we are talking about.

Here the entire meaning of the blessing, the empowerment, or the initiation that we receive is the understanding of this and the capacity to practice this. All of the subject matter of the scripture pertains to this. It is all about selflessness. It is all about the Natural Mind. Don't think that there is some other subject besides that which is being pointed out now.

In other contexts, there would be much to discuss about mind in terms of main minds, mental factors, ordinary mind, and transcendent mind. None of that discussion is relevant here. This is all about the Natural Mind, the inseparability of primordial purity and the spontaneous presence of all qualities. It is all about recognizing the Natural Mind and the method of practicing it, which leads to enlightenment. Practice means learning and listening and discussing, these are all part of the practice, but of particular importance is that we need to have inner experience.

Satrig Ersang Supplication

ying-kyi yum chen-mo sa-trig er-sang ni
Great Mother of the Sphere, Satrig Ersang,

ku-dog ser-gyi nying-po dra
color like the essence of gold,

gyen-dang cha-lug zhe-ye-kang
her ornaments, clothing, and mandala mansion

ser-la ser-gyi ö-kyi rab-tu dze-par gyen
are golden and adorned by golden light.

chag-tsen ye-na ser-gyi yi-ge pa-wo dru-nga nam
In her right hand she holds the five brave golden letters.

chag-tsen yön-na nang-sel ser-gyi me-long nam
In her left hand she holds a shining golden mirror.

rin-po-che tar tra-wa-yi tsel-chen seng-ge nyi-kyi tri-la zhug
Beautiful as a jewel, she sits on a throne of two powerful lions.

jin-gyi lab-kyi dro-way dön-dze-pay
By her blessings she provides for the welfare of living beings.

sa-trig er-sang ku-la chag-tsel-lo
Prostration to the Body of Satrig Ersang!

Satrig Ersang, the Great Mother

Satrig Ersang

Homage to the Principal Dakini of the Five Sets of Dakinis!

Great Mother Satrig Ersang emanated a beautiful samaya-dakini, Dzema Yiwongma, who taught these blessed instructions of the female lineage to the goddesses (walmo) and dakinis. All those of the female lineage were satisfied and cleared of doubts. The samaya-dakini Dzema Yiwongma plucked the written instructions from space in ink of lapis lazuli written on copper sheets, blessed it, and gave it to them. The Indian Dakini Ulishag translated them into Sanskrit. The meaning is presented in two aspects: direct demonstration of the non-verbal signs; and verbal explanation of all the meanings as being included within Natural Mind.

As we have been discussing, the Great Mother Satrig Ersang is the basis of all the awakened beings, all of the enlightened Goddesses. She, the Great Mother, emanated as a Dakini Damstig Khandro, and in order to give the instructions to the Dakinis, she took from space a sheet of copper with writing in blue lapis lazuli ink. On the basis of that, she gave these instructions. She gave all these to an Indian Dakini (Khandro) named Ulishak who translated them into Sanskrit. It's from this that we have the practice.

1. Dakini Dzema Yiwongma

No. 1 Dakini Dzema Yiwongma

Samaya-Dakini Dzema Yiwongma showed the Indian Dakini Ulishak

Sign number 1: a rope of light in space.

Meaning 1: This primordially existent bodhicitta-dharmakaya lacks the five aggregates; it is beyond flourishing and declining, birth and death, joining and separating; it cannot be killed or destroyed. All existence is included within Natural Mind, primordially abiding within dharmakaya. From the mind-transmission vidhyadhara lineage, it was then passed on to the worldly deities.

Thus she spoke.

The First Dakini, Samaya-Dakini, gave these teachings to the Indian Dakini Ulishak, first by revealing a sign and then explaining its meaning. Sometimes the signs used in transmissions of the Lineage were not spoken, but were nonverbal communications. In each case there was some kind of sign that was revealed, then the meaning of that was explained. The first sign that the Dakini showed was "a rope of light in space." What is the meaning of this? The meaning of it is the Dharmakaya, in this context referred to as the Bonku (*bon sku*). It is Bodhichitta, the Natural Mind we were referring to before. The text says this primordial Bonku or Bodhichitta is free from the five aggregates. It knows neither youth nor old age, neither increase, nor decrease; it is beyond birth and death, and so on. Out of the three bodies—Dharmakaya, Sambhogakaya and Nirmanakaya, this is the Dharmakaya or Bonku. It does not get better or worse. That is because it is not bound by the five

Samsaric aggregates of form, feeling, perception, concept, and consciousness. Therefore, it has no increase or decrease. It does not improve or degenerate. Unlike ordinary people, animals and impermanent things, which are born, produce and grow, and eventually degenerate and pass away, the Bonku (Dharmakaya) is unborn and unceasing. There was never a point when it began and neither is there a time when it disintegrates or disappears. The text goes on to say that since it is beyond birth and death, it is beyond amalgamation and disintegration, as it has never been something that can be destroyed. All appearances and whatever exists are within the mind and abide in the dimension of primordial Bonku. It is the source of all appearances and existence. As it is said, "Homage to the Great Mother from which all phenomena arise, in which all phenomenon abide, and into which all phenomenon dissolve."

Bonku is that from which all phenomena arise, abide in and dissolve back into. Appearances are always within it; they always abide within it. They are never separate from it nor do they ever go outside of Bonku. They arise from it, abide in it and dissolve back into it.

2. Dakini Ulishak

No. 2 Dakini Ulishag

The Indian Dakini Ulishag revealed to Dakini Goddess Namkha Ökyi Gyelmo

Sign number 2: palms bursting forth in space.

Meaning 2. Because it is ultimately unending within the non-declining victory banner of Bodhicitta-Natural-Mind, Dharmakaya is without increase or decrease; it is changeless; it is the great indestructible yung-drung of the three times, a primordial victory banner that does not abandon the root basis of samsara and nirvana.

Thus she spoke.

This Bonku, this Dharmakaya, this Natural Mind that we are talking about, does not improve or become better. It remains as it has always been. It is the same material that it has always been. It does not increase or decrease. It does not change. The symbol of the Yung Drung (swastika) means it is immutable, unchanging in the past, present and future. The pristine banner of victory is primordially free from the extremes of samsara or nirvana. The symbolism of the victory banner is that it is something that never sets, never disappears. It never ceases to exist. It is unceasing and it also has the sense of being victorious. It is the very basis of both samsara and nirvana, and is never destroyed. Remember now that these are all characteristics and qualities of the Natural Mind that we are talking about. The same single sphere is the nature of reality, the Natural Mind, Bodhichitta, and Dharmakaya. All of these descriptions pertain to this single subject, upon which all of this is focused.

3. Dakini Namkha Ökyi Gyelmo

No. 3 Dakini Namkha Ökyi Gyelmo

Dakini Goddess Namkha Ökyi Gyelmo revealed to Dakini Salwa Yingchug Ma of Razhag

Sign number 3: Her body standing in space.

Meaning 3: The defining characteristic of Natural Mind is being primordially enlightened. That Yung-Drung-Bodhicitta is beyond thought, causes and conditions. Leaving body and mind unaltered, arise in the singular Dharmakaya, free from extremes of appearance and Emptiness; the primordially self-arising body.

Thus she spoke.

Then the Third Dakini, also known as Walmoza, passed on instructions to the Dakini Razhagza Salwa Yingchyugma. The sign that she passed on means that the nature of mind has been forever enlightened. It is primordially free from causes and conditions.

Causes and conditions indicate some kind of process or effort that is being applied. For there to be some result dependent upon a cause, there needs to be some kind of transformation or change that takes place. For instance, a flower has its cause in the seed that is planted. There are two kinds of causes. There are the primary causes that go into the actual substance of the effect, like the seed which becomes the flower. Then there are the secondary causes, such as the contributing conditions of the water, the soil, the fertilizer, the sun, and so on. These are the two types of causes that go into the production of the flower. Ordinary minds have causal conditions like seeing an object, and that gives rise to pleasant or unpleasant feelings, and then to labeling the object as good or bad, or so on. Ordinary minds have different kinds of causal conditions that go into their production.

Some teachers of Dzogchen explain Natural Mind in a similar way, as involving causes and conditions, but in this case it is not at all that way. It is free from conceptual thought. It is already beyond thought, beyond concepts. We have thoughts just like we have a body. Natural Mind is not affected by your body and it is not affected by conceptual thoughts. It is the Yung Drung (swastika) Bodhichitta. Yung Drung means it is immutable, unchanging, and in talking about Natural Mind, it is isolated from body and mind. Neither the body nor ordinary mind can affect it. What we are saying here is that these different kinds of appearances do not harm it. They arise from it, abide within it, and dissolve back into it.

The Natural Mind is not harmed or affected by ordinary mind. Sometimes this is a point that is discussed and debated with logic. Basically, we are saying that the Natural Mind is beyond the ordinary body, speech and mind. However, the ordinary body, speech and mind are not beyond Natural Mind. They are contained within it. That is the big difference. This is the dimension of the nature of mind in which objects of meditation are liberated into the Natural State.

It is said that appearances and emptiness are inseparable. It is not just empty. It is not just clarity. When we say clarity, we think of the clear light mind, the pure Natural Mind. Neither one of these are separate; it is both and inseparable. It is both emptiness and clear light. It is said to be the self-arising body. It is not something that has been created by a producer. It is not something that has been attained through the accumulation of merit and wisdom and developed on that basis. It has always been self-arising.

4. Dakini Selwa Yingchug Ma

No. 4 Dakini Salwa Yingchug Ma

Dakini Salwa Yingchug Ma of Razhag revealed to Dakini Ökyi Lama of Zhangzhung

Sign number 4: pulling at the nape of her neck with her right hand fingers.

Meaning 4: Primordially unobscured, Natural Mind is empty and clear. By mind looking at mind, appearing objects are exhausted. Then, settle in a state beyond observed objects, with nothing to see. This is the empty space of the mind; objects of meditation are released within pristine Awareness.

Thus she spoke.

Natural Mind has never been obscured by imprints or appearances, but it has the two characteristics of being empty and illuminating. If anger arises in our mind and we look at its very entity, then it disappears. What do you find, when you look at and focus on something special? Nothing. Some texts talk about it being like space; just an empty vacuity. When you focus on that empty vacuity, then you are finding the Natural Mind. Whatever it was that caused your anger, the object of your annoyance, you do not need to keep it in mind. You do not need to focus on it. The object of meditation is released to pure awareness; naturally liberated, automatically released. This is the way we meditate. This is the way that daily problems can evaporate, can be dissipated. If we talk about recognizing Natural Mind, this is how it is done. This is the basic procedure that we will be following to meditate on Natural Mind. It is just this kind of process. When there is an object arising in the mind, an object of anger, look directly at the entity of the anger, find nothing to hold on to, nothing to grasp, nothing but empty space, and then settle into equipoise and focus on that. That is how we meditate on the Natural Mind.

5. Dakini Ökyi Lama

No. 5 Dakini Ökyi Lama

Dakini Ökyi Lama of Zhangzhung showed the Lady of the Dong family, Dakini Kharmokyong

Sign number 5: the automatic stopping of thought.

Meaning 5: Space is an example for Natural Mind. The meaning exemplified is being primordially awakened. Emptiness and clarity, unconditioned, Pure Awareness pervades all from center to edges. Dharmakaya is empty, beyond inherently existent objects. Settle, integrating with Pure Awareness, on the basis of whatever appears.

Thus she spoke.

The fourth and the fifth transmission are actually quite similar. The example is the sky. The meaning is that Natural Mind is primordially enlightened. In general, the Natural Mind is beyond symbols and beyond signs. But speaking of signs and symbols can indicate a kind of approach to it and gives us a kind of path by which we can reach it. Therefore, we have this example of space, the sky. The meaning is that it is primordially enlightened. We create a lot of karma, but as explained before, this can not harm or affect Natural Mind.

If we have the experience of Natural Mind, then it is very easy to be released from karma. As opposed to implementing different kinds of antidotes and methods by which to purify karma and be free of karma's cause and effect, focusing upon Natural Mind and experiencing Natural Mind in meditation is much faster for bringing that about. You can pursue purification and accumulation of positive energy through recitation of mantras, or meditation on deities and making offerings, but Dzogchen meditation focusing on Natural Mind is a much more powerful way for bringing that about. That is because all appearances arise from, abide in, and dissolve back into Natural Mind. It is the same with karma. It is therefore easier to release karma into Natural Mind. This is why we say that in Natural Mind we are primordially enlightened.

Natural Mind pervades all phenomena. Unlike ordinary intelligence, this nonduality of emptiness and spontaneous accomplishment is referred to in Tibetan as *Rigpi Yeshe*, timeless wisdom of pure awareness. Natural Mind is beyond all conventional phenomena that appear to living beings—like forms to the eyes, sounds to the ears, smells to the nose, tastes to the tongue, feelings to the body. Can we abide in this Natural Mind that is beyond all conventionally grasped objects? Yes, we can. We can settle and relax into it because we have never really been separate from it. In general, our assertion is that it is beginningless. We have forever been inseparable from it and this will continue into the future as well. That is why we can abide in it. That is why we can understand it and realize it. That's why we can definitely dispel and clear mental afflictions or problems into it.

One line gives us our meditation instructions: "No matter what appearances arise, settle and integrate them into Intrinsic Awareness." This does not mean we have to stop them or prevent them from arising. We do not do that, whatever appearances arise. Externally, it could be a bright sunny day or pouring cats and dogs, or, in the case of our mental state, we may be happy or sad; it doesn't make any difference. Looking directly at it, we will arrive at the Natural State, just like clouds clearing to reveal the sky. There is a big difference here in this method. If we consciously or intentionally stop appearances, we do not arrive at the Natural State. When it says that no matter what appearances arise, settle and integrate them into Intrinsic Awareness, that is very different from saying no matter what appearances arise, stop them and settle. No, when appearances arise, we settle into the Natural Mind.

There are different ways of meditating. For instance, in the middle way, Madhyamaka, emptiness is meditated upon by ceasing or stopping conventional appearance. There is a big difference there. Here there is no stopping the appearances; just settling into the Natural State. We should meditate like this.

6. Dakini Kharmokyong

No. 6 Dakini Kharmokyong

The Lady Dong, Dakini Kharmokyong, showed Dakini Mang-je Salgye-ö of Persia

Sign number 6: light in space.

Meaning 6: When we examine Natural Mind, whatever appears is primordially pure. Since natural appearances are released, this is nondual dharmakaya. All of existence is liberated, not rejected; this is supreme awakening. Whatever happens in appearances is manifestation of Pure Awareness.

Thus she spoke.

When we analyze Natural Mind in terms of its function, in terms of what arises from it, we realize that whatever appears is primordially pure. What we find is something that is empty. Just like ice may appear different than water, when it melts it is no different from the water. When appearances arise in your mind and you examine them, they dissolve back into the Natural State. You see that they were none other than the Natural State of the mind of pure awareness. As you examine them, they are released and liberated into the Natural Mind.

We may have all sorts of thoughts arise in our mind, pleasant feelings or painful feelings, but when we look at them, they have no place left to go. They dissolve right back into the Natural State, nondual from it. It is just as if you pour water into water, or like wind blowing through the sky—look at those thoughts and they disappear. We lose them in the space of the Natural Mind. In the case of unpleasant feelings or anger rising in our mind, they arise out of the Natural Mind. They have no other basis, no other foundation than the Natural Mind itself.

Naturally, there is no other place for them to go. When water with silt in it is stirred up, it looks cloudy. If it is allowed to settle and be still, then the silt falls to the bottom and the water appears clear. When the mind is left undisturbed and those silt-like concepts are allowed to settle, then ultimate liberation can be attained. When this happens, it is not that the thoughts and concepts are dispelled or gotten rid of when liberation is attained. It is that in knowing their nature they are released and liberation is attained.

The last line of the meaning of this sign is very powerful. Dongcham Kharmokyong said to Tazigza Manggye Salgyema that "Whatever happens in appearances is manifestation of Pure Awareness." This is the nature of all appearances in the mind; they are the manifestation or energy of pure awareness. There is no need to get rid of them. There is no need to do anything with them. They are a manifestation of pure transcendent wisdom itself. No matter what painful feeling you have and whatever you think—if you think "Oh, I'm stupid," or if any kind of delusion arises in the mind—you don't need to be concerned about it because it is just a manifestation of your own pure wisdom awareness. If you try to use some other method to get rid of this worry, this painful feeling or thought, it just gets worse. If another thought is needed as an antidote, then that process will be unending and there will be another reason and another background, and then that thought, again, would need another support and another...and so it becomes unending. It is like you are shooting one pool ball at another, hoping to sink the first ball. It is not going to work. It is going to hit a ball and that ball is going to ricochet and hit another one, and then you have a chain reaction. The kind of release that we are talking about is a natural release; whatever feelings or thoughts arise are naturally liberated. Like a snake that is coiled into a knot, if someone else comes along and tries to untie the knot, it is a little difficult. But the snake can easily unwind its own knots. That is how this release happens. If you understand the Natural Mind, this empty luminosity becomes like a house that is empty for a thief. A thief comes in and sees there is nothing there to steal, so does not come anymore.

We have the six consciousnesses, the five sense consciousnesses along with mental consciousness, and all have a function. The visual consciousness perceives objects. Auditory consciousness hears sounds. Olfactory consciousness smells. Tongue consciousness tastes and physical body feels. The mental consciousness thinks and is aware of things. Once we understand the Natural State, then these consciousnesses continue to function, but without grasping onto the reality of what they perceive. When that happens, no more karmic predispositions are created. As in the last line of this instruction, whatever appearances arise in the mind are established to be the Natural State of the mind, the Natural Mind itself, the energy of the Natural Mind itself arising. Then karma is not created anymore and great liberation will be attained.

By becoming very certain that whatever appears in your mind, whatever activities your body, speech and mind engage in, are the very manifestations or energy of your own Natural Mind, then everything becomes practice. Everything becomes a part of practice, or a support of practice. Singing or doing physical activities—all of them are realized to be manifestations of the Natural Mind. Thinking becomes an activity in which there is no grasping involved. This is something very important for us to understand. It is a way of transforming all of our activities into practice. We do not get that much time for formal practice. We have to spend a lot of our time working, talking, and doing different things. Maintaining the awareness that this is all the energy of my own enlightened mind, it is all Natural Mind manifesting, is a useful practice for us because then all of our daily activities can be transformed into practice.

First of all, it is important for us to have an intellectual understanding of this. Secondly, we need to have conviction that this is the case, to believe that this is true. This conviction or belief is not to be derived simply from reading the text and saying "Oh, that's the way it is," but through our own practice and experience. Coming to understand this develops the deep conviction within us. This goes beyond just having conviction in this particular Guru Yoga or whatever instruction, but having the conviction in the Natural State itself, knowing that your own Natural Mind is the transcendent wisdom awareness and having deep conviction in it.

7. Dakini Mang-je Salgye-ö

No. 7 Dakini Mang-je Salgye-ö

Dakini Mang-je Salgye-ö of Persia showed the lower caste Dakini Dutsi-kyong of Uddiyana

Sign number 7: her arms embracing her thighs.

Meaning 7: In the space of Natural Mind, primordially empty, all-pervasive, arise its mudra-manifestations, mandalas, forms and colors. They never move outside of the mind's ultimate nature. Not moving out of the mind's true nature is the seal of Natural Mind.

Thus she spoke.

Primarily, this describes how appearances arise within emptiness, such as the four elements and sentient beings, as well as enlightened beings, their abodes and mandalas. Where are they? They are in emptiness. This is just like saying, where are the moon and all the stars? They are in space. All phenomena exist within ultimate nature, selflessness and emptiness. We might think this is like empty space, but it is not. Empty space is an ordinary emptiness because it does not have the qualities of wisdom and illumination. Mere empty space does not have the capacity to give rise to appearances. All the many varieties and aspects of meditational deities such as the Great Mother Choza Bonmo, the Great Mother Perfection of Wisdom, with all of her colors and ornaments—all of these arise within selflessness or emptiness. It is the Natural Mind that has the power to give rise to all of the enlightened qualities, i.e., realized qualities and activities of body, speech and mind. All of these are the manifestations of the transcendent wisdom awareness of Natural Mind.

In this way, this emptiness that we are talking about is not just an empty vacuity exactly like space; space is only used as an example. It is exalted above that. All the realized qualities are spontaneously present within it. When we talk about emptiness here, you need not worry that we are talking about just some emptiness where there is nothingness, or something like that. Rather it has all of the spontaneously present awakened qualities including, for instance, the sixty perfections. There is a set of six perfections, and a set of ten, and they can be multiplied to get sixty by subdividing them. For example, with the perfection of generosity, there is the generosity of generosity, the discipline of generosity, the patience of generosity, the effort of generosity, the concentration of generosity, and the wisdom of generosity, not to mention, then, the methods of generosity, the prayers of generosity, the power of generosity and the transcendent wisdom of generosity. All of the six or the ten perfections can be subdivided like that. All of these are permutations of the perfections and the sixty aspects are spontaneously present within Natural Mind.

Each of these instructions were given individually by one woman to another, by one Dakini to the next. But all of them are dealing with our one subject, the specific characteristics of emptiness which is full of potential, this Natural Mind.

8. Dakini Dutsi-kyong

No. 8 Dakini Dutsi-kyong

Dakini Dutsi-kyong of Uddiyana showed the Indian Dakini Thuchen of Phamting

Sign number 8: moving down and pressing with her hand.

Meaning 8: Since Natural Mind is not objectifiable, Dharmakaya is beyond effort. It has no color, no shape, no dimensions. Since it is primordially beyond production and disintegration it cannot be destroyed by anything. Abide in objectless spaciousness, empty and all-pervasive.

Thus she spoke.

When we talk about Natural Mind or true nature, Bonku or Dharmakaya, these are all referring to the same thing. The nature of mind is objectless. It is beyond duality, it transcends duality. It is beyond conventional effort being applied. When you abide in it, it is effortless. This is taught so that we understand that the meditation is not fabricated; it is not one with effort. It is precisely because Natural Mind is beyond all conventional effort that you pay attention to it. The reason we need to look at it, meditate on it, is in order to understand that the appearances that arise originate from it. Once we have understood and realized Natural Mind, then it brings an end to our trials and tribulations. If some intense anger arises in your mind, when you have a strong understanding that it is Natural Mind manifesting that emotion or thought, then it can be released very quickly, dissolved instantly. Just as if you suffer a shooting pain in your body, you take medicine to relieve it and the pain disappears.

The nature of Natural Mind is free of color, shape, size, and objects. It is not like a conventional object. This is because it is not form; therefore it has no color, shape, size, and so on. As far as the size of this Natural Mind, a statement in the text of the *Twenty-one Nails* says it is the size of your first thumb joint. But really, that is a symbol for something that does not get smaller or bigger. It is described as fixed at a particular size, but that does not mean that it has an actual size. You cannot take everything you read in the scriptures literally. Sharza Rinpoche said that the understanding you can amass from reading heaps of scriptures is not like the one that you receive directly from the spiritual master. This is making the point that you cannot take all the scriptures literally and think that you understand them. That is just a diversion.

Seriously speaking, there are two kinds of meanings expressed in the scriptures. One is provisional, a meaning that is intended to take one deeper. Then there are other meanings that are ultimate and definitive; what is being said is what is actually meant. In a provisional teaching, one thing is said but you understand something else. For example, why would Buddha say something if it were not to be taken literally? There are some people who became Buddha's disciples who were previously non-Buddhist. He gave them some teachings that corresponded to their non-Buddhist philosophy. It was not Buddha's ultimate thought, idea, understanding or realization of how things are. But if you do not know how to explain this well, there are mistakes that could be made with this presentation. It is because of this that many different kinds of commentarial traditions developed on the basis of the great trailblazers of the Mahayana, Asanga and Nagarjuna's systems. The Indian and Tibetan commentators on their systems came up with a lot of different ways of explaining the teachings because of the fact that there are both provisional as well as definitive teachings.

The same goes for Dzogchen scriptures. There are teachings in Dzogchen scriptures that are provisional and then there are others that are definitive. For instance, in most of the Dzogchen scriptures there is not a presentation of the two truths, conventional and ultimate truth or conventional and ultimate nature of phenomenon. But in some Dzogchen scriptures there are. The explanation of two natures, conventional and ultimate, corresponds to the Madhyamaka Middle Way presentation for people who are familiar with that and who are going into Dzogchen practice. This is an explanation for the student's capacity of understanding and provides incremental instruction.

The Natural Mind is primordial, unborn, and indestructible. It cannot be liberated by any antidote. Nothing can destroy it, nor was it ever born. It is a case of getting to the most subtle level of the mind. There are grosser levels, subtler levels, and then the subtlest level of mind. Reaching the subtlest level of the mind is like going through the nine vehicles. You start off with a certain view, then it progresses to a more refined view and philosophy, up until you reach the ninth one where you reach the subtlest of views, the subtlest state of mind. Once you reach that, there is nothing above it, there is nothing that can negate it. There is nothing that can act as an antidote to it. The effort that is applied in these successive vehicles becomes less and less. It becomes a subtler and subtler kind of effort being applied, until it becomes effortless.

In the practices of the foundation six perfections, both the philosophy and the conduct require a great deal of effort to be applied. At the Dzogchen level, both the view or the philosophy and the conduct have reached its subtlest level. Conduct is said to be one in which there is no adoption or rejection.

9. Dakini Thuchen

No. 9 Dakini Thuchen

The Indian Dakini Thuchen of Phamting showed the Chinese Dakini Selwa Ödrön

Sign number 9: transference of consciousness into a wrathful Deity.

Meaning 9: Since existence is the shining of pure luminosity that far exceeds a thousand suns and moons, dwelling in all pervasive luminosity dispels the darkness of ignorance. Since it is primordially enlightened, samsara is completely uprooted. Since its previous and later qualities are not different, the three times are of one nature.

Thus she spoke.

It is something for us to imagine what one thousand suns or one thousand moons would be like. The idea of extreme brilliance and Intrinsic Awareness is even brighter than that. Entire realms of existence and appearances are arising. All that exists and all that appears, arises from transcendent wisdom awareness, the Natural Mind. It is the quality of clear light illumination.

When we talk about the light of the sun and the moon, that is an ordinary kind of light. The kind of light we are talking about here is the light of the Natural Mind, the light of all appearance. No matter how bright the light of the sun and the moon is, it cannot dispel the darkness of the ignorance within ourselves. Whereas, this clear light of the Natural Mind can easily clear away the darkness of ignorance, no matter how dark or dense it has become. It is just as if a cave has been in darkness for hundreds of thousands of years, but the moment you bring one candle inside, you can instantly see it all. Our meditation becomes like this. It is not just for pacifying or making our mind calm, but it has a quality of illumination we call clear light. That is why we consider our meditation or view to be like illuminating clear light. Because it has the nature of clear light, it can purify and clear away all the darkness, ignorance, delusion and obscurations.

Clear light is all pervasive. It does not pervade some things or some phenomena and not others. It pervades both samsara and nirvana. If we do not use this particular terminology, we can say it pervades all that is positive and all that is negative. It pervades all happiness and all suffering. By remaining in this great pervasive clarity, the darkness of ignorance is cleared away. Realizing the Natural Mind up-ends and completely reverses samara. Samsara is only a temporary condition, whereas Buddhahood is eternal; it has forever been Buddha. We have two syllables in Tibetan for the word Buddha, which is *sang gye*. The first syllable, *sang*, means purified. It means that it has been forever pure of defilements. The second syllable, *gye*, means expanded. It means that all positive qualities, all transcendent wisdom, have always been fully developed and are spontaneously present. When we understand our primordial condition, that we have been forever enlightened, then samsara ceases. It cannot harm us or cause us grief. Since there is no separation into past and future, the three times are essentially one in Natural Mind. Samsara and its defilements of ignorance, delusions and karma are like some smelly clothes that we put on, which can be taken off; whereas Natural Mind is forever the same, past present and future, pure and uncontaminated.

This Natural Mind is the same for us and all the Buddhas. Many beings in the past have attained Buddhahood because they have identified and recognized Natural Mind within themselves, practiced and manifested it. Otherwise, the material they had to work with is no different than which is within us. It is because of this that these beings are called awakened beings or Buddhas. If we undertake this kind of teaching in order to understand the Natural State and, once we recognize it, identify it and practice it, then we will also become a fully enlightened being. It is not that the Natural Mind within us has improved. It is that our practice has improved, has developed. The Natural Mind itself is primordially pure and spontaneously accomplished and has been intact from the beginning. It does not get better or worse.

Enlightenment is not something for us to believe in, something far away in the distance or in the future. It is merely something for us to realize as present, only obscured by clouds. Sometimes there may be more clouds and at other times there are fewer clouds. They are easily cleared away. There will definitely be a progression in that direction when we meditate, practice and develop experience. We can understand how this happens through our own experience once we get familiar with the practice. This kind of development of practice is found when we have been meditating for any length of time. There is a progression. Meditation is about accustoming oneself. In Tibetan, the word *gom* means familiarizing, accustoming, getting used to something. We will definitely develop in our understanding of this, not only in formal meditation practice, but also as we carry it into our daily life. It is the understanding that appearances and activities are the manifestations of the Natural State of Dharmakaya. It is something that is not very difficult. Once you have this recognition of the Natural State, then it is just a matter of bringing it to mind, remembering it. Whether you are walking, making food, or whatever.

10. Dakini Selwa Ödrön

No. 10 Dakini Selwa Ödrön

The Chinese Dakini Selwa Ödrön showed the Dakini Drimé Dangden Ma of Yorpo

Sign number 10: transference of consciousness into base-clear-light, Natural Mind.

Meaning 10: Natural Mind is the nature of great nectar. Since it enjoys everything within and without, whatever appears is nectar. Since it seals whatever appears, Natural Mind is the supreme of nectars. Since it pervades immeasurable space, Dharmakaya is nectar.

Thus she spoke.

What is meant here by nectar, ambrosia or *dutsi*, is something very powerful. In Tibetan *dutsi* literally means the destroyer of Mara or evil. To give an example, it is like something you could give to a dying person that would prevent them from dying. It has that kind of power. There are different kinds of Mara meant here by the word '*du*,' or the Mara that is destroyed. One meaning of Mara, is the Lord of Death, referring to death itself. The word *tsi*, literally means the sap or essence of a medicine, but it does not necessarily have to indicate that. It could mean anything that has the function of destroying mara, or death. Many kinds of maras exist. What is being said here is that for somebody who recognizes or identifies the Natural State within themselves, and practices it, there is nothing that is not included within that—everything is like nectar. All phenomena are enjoyed like they are ambrosia. Whether phenomena are internal or external, they are nectar. The Natural State can be used to clear, to purify all the daily kinds of sufferings and unpleasant experiences that we have. It can also be used to purify negative karma. It can also be used as the nectar which heals the fears and dangers that arise in the intermediate state at the time after death when our old body has been discarded, and before we have connected with a new body. This is called the *bardo*, in Tibetan. There are many kinds of frightening experiences that can arise in the bardo and this practice is a medicine that heals and protects from those kinds of dangers and frights.

It can also be used for the ultimate attainment, the attainment of full enlightenment. This is called self-awareness because it has its own awareness that transcends ordinary mind and activity as clear light. We mentioned before that clear light pervades all phenomena, just like the sun when it rises over an area illuminates the entire area clearly. If you focus on that clear light, it dispels unknowing ignorance. Here it is saying that it pervades ignorance and delusions. This means that it clears it away, and it clears the way. That supreme nectar of all nectars is our own transcendent wisdom awareness, the Natural Mind. That is the nectar we call the *Bonku*, Dharmakaya.

11. Dakini Drimé Dangden Ma

No. 11 Dakini Drimé Dangden Ma

Dakini Drimé Dangden Ma of Yorpo showed the Dakini of the Cho family, Ökyi Dzutrul Tön

Sign number 11: right hand lifting the right knee.

Meaning 11: Natural Mind is like space; it is primordially empty, selfless, and all-pervasive. Natural Mind is like a lotus; it is free from extremes of good and bad, both outside and inside. Natural Mind is like a jewel treasure; whatever is wished or needed arises from it. Natural Mind is like a rainbow; it is the Dharmakaya of non-dual appearance and Emptiness.

Thus she spoke.

Some of these signs, in dependence upon which the transmissions were passed on, are rather obvious. Others of these nonverbal gestures are more difficult for us to understand. It is also difficult, sometimes, to know exactly what they looked like. In this case, Dakini Drimé Dangden Ma of Yorpo passed the instructions to Dakini of the Cho family, Ökyi Dzutrul Tön. These particular names are Tibetan, and therefore, these Dakinis can be identified as Tibetan women.

In all these cases, the meaning of the transmission is that which we experience in Natural Mind meditation, in Dzogchen meditation. There are symbols by which we can comprehend and receive some indication of what we can experience in Dzogchen.

There is much that can appear to us in our experience. There is the factor of appearance, the factor of emptiness, and the factor of the union of those two. Sometimes it seems to us that Natural Mind is a factor of appearance and sometimes it seems like it is a factor of emptiness. Sometimes we have uncertainty about it, we do not understand how there is a complete unification of these two. It will appear in various and different ways, as appearance or as emptiness, but the fact of the matter is that they are in union.

Natural Mind is like space, Dharmakaya. It is like space in the sense that it has infinitely pervaded all phenomena. Natural Mind is like a lotus. The lotus grows out of mud and muck into a form that is beautiful in shape, color and fragrance. In a similar way, Natural Mind is free of all faults, outer or inner. Natural Mind is also like a precious jewel. It is really like a treasury, a king's treasury of precious things. Or you can think of it as an inexhaustible mine of jewels that exists in the ground beneath you. This symbolizes how all of the qualities of the enlightened state, compassion and timeless wisdom, all derive from Natural Mind.

The Natural Mind is like a rainbow because it manifests in many various colors. The rainbow symbolizes that Natural Mind will appear to you in your practice of meditation in many different ways. Sometimes it will appear as great emptiness, sometimes it will appear as rays of light. This indicates the variety of appearances. This particular transmission introduces us to these different qualities or characteristics of Natural Mind. If it is explained in an extensive way, all the instructions are included within it.

12. Dakini Ökyi Dzutrul Tön

No. 12 Dakini Ökyi Dzutrul Tön

The Dakini of the Cho family, Ökyi Dzutrul Tön, showed the Dakini Dzutrul Natsog Tön of Drusha

Sign number 12: six wheels of light.

Meaning 12: Natural Mind lacks inherent existence and is free from the extreme of permanence. Since it is never missing, it is free from the extreme of nihilism. It does not cling to the six objects of consciousness, and is free from self-grasping. It is beyond color and direction, free from all clinging to inherent existence.

Thus she spoke.

The nature of mind is free from extremes. There are many ways that extremes can be categorized, such as the eight extremes, four extremes, or two extremes. One symbol for this freedom from extremes is waving a spear in space. When a long spear is waving, there is absolutely no obstruction in space. Sometimes this is the explanation of this commentary simply for the sake of developing understanding, looking at the extremes of existence, non-existence, permanence, and impermanence.

Scholars give commentaries on these, but in fact it is impossible to explain these extremes. You can say emptiness is permanent, but permanence is merely a label that is placed upon it. Natural Mind is actually free from the extreme of permanence; it is beyond permanence. Another symbol used is a *phurpa* (Tib.), a peg or stake stuck into the loose mud where you can move it around. It symbolizes how it is not fixed in one position. It is free from extremes. It is like a rubber band that can stretch out in any direction. It is not limited. The emptiness of Natural Mind is vast. It is not at all limited. It is free and open. It is free from extremes. You can discuss these things and analyze them in terms of being free from the extremes, but the essence of it is just as described. We do not need to go into this analytical process. Although analysis can be applied by looking at these extremes, when that is done, it is done on the basis of a subject-object duality. It is the analysis of what is being observed and what is the observer, what are the subject and object. Because of that, it does not really correspond to the meaning, which is nonduality. So it does not exactly further one's practice by having this dualistic kind of analysis.

Since Natural Mind does not grasp at the six specific objects, it is free from clinging to the concept of self. When self-grasping ignorance develops, it is on the basis of the appearance of the six objects, the five sense objects and the one mental object. Natural Mind is free from grasping at the six objects. It is free from all grasping. This transmission is primarily in regard to Natural Mind being free from all extremes.

13. Dakini Dzutrul Natsog Tön

No. 13 Dakini Dzutrul Natsog Tön

The Dakini Dzutrul Natsog Tön of Drusha showed the Lung-gyen Dakini Nangwa Datön Ma

Sign number 13: a union of lights of method and wisdom.

Meaning 13: Within the Great Permanence of absence of meeting and parting, liberation and deception, there is the spontaneously established Great Nihilism absent of ego grasping. Since existence is self-sealed, it is the Great Self. Since existence is true nature appearing, it is the Great Grasping of Reality

Thus, she spoke.

The meaning of this transmission is actually similar to the previous one. When you look at the words of the instruction, it looks like it is the exact opposite of what was just said, but in fact the meaning is the same. It is to indicate that the Natural Mind is beyond saying it is one way or another, that it is like this, or not like that. So, using the exact opposite terminology indicates that Natural Mind is beyond these kinds of designations as being this or that, not this or not that.

It is said that the Natural Mind is the Great Permanence or Great Eternalism. To state that it is free from meeting and parting, or liberation and deception, means it is not perceived as one or as things gathered and collected into one. Nor is it seen as separate or distinct. For example, a person and their aggregates are not seen as one with those aggregates nor as separate from the aggregates.

Natural Mind is free from liberation and deception in the sense that it is not going to be liberated in the future. It has always been liberated. This kind of teaching is called Great Permanence. The text says, "there is spontaneously established Great Nihilism absent of ego grasping." Normally, Natural Mind is said to be free from the extremes of permanence or nihilism. In this case, from the point of view of being forever free of grasping at the reality of things, nihilism is spontaneous—meaning it is forever free from grasping reality.

The instructions state, "Since existence is self-sealed, it is the Great Self." The word self is used in varying contexts to mean different things. On the one hand, we speak of the self as myself or others, which is merely imputed, merely a label that is put on one person who passes from one lifetime to the next. It is just a term that designates the conventional reality of a person who passes from one life to the next. On the other hand, the word self is used to describe that which is negated in the teachings: the self that is propounded or asserted by non-Buddhist philosophies as one that is inherently, independently self-existent. In this case, that kind of self is negated in the teachings.

But the word self is used in other ways also. Here, the Natural Mind is being called the "Great Self" because it seals all existence and appearances. Natural Mind has its stamp on all appearances and existence. Conventionally speaking, when we talk about the self, it is the owner of the aggregates, for example, "my mind, my body, my feelings" and so on. Similar to the designation of the self as being the one that is in charge of the aggregates of a person, here the Natural Mind is designated as the Great Self because it pervades and leaves its stamp or seal upon everything that exists.

Generally speaking, the view or the philosophy in Dzogchen

practice does correspond to the teachings of Buddha, the perfections and so on, and Buddha's explanation of the absence of self. In general, that is the view that is accepted in the context of the Dzogchen and other Tibetan traditions as well.

14. Dakini Dakini Nangwa Datön Ma

No. 14 Dakini Nangwa Datön Ma

The Lung-gyen Dakini Nangwa Datön Ma showed the Dakini Tog-beb Ma of Menyag ancestry

Sign number 14: squatting like a dog or lion, gazing into space.

Meaning 14: Not rejecting appearances of light, they are recognized as manifestations of Pure Awareness. Any grasping conceptions that arise are the playground of Pure Awareness. Not thinking about what appears, it is Pure Awareness's place of liberation. Primordially not thinking of anything is the resultant Liberation.

Thus she spoke.

There is no need to guard, or worry about, what kind of appearances come to mind. You will have various experiences—pleasant appearances, unpleasant appearances, good experiences, and bad experiences. The instruction is to not worry or be too concerned about what kinds of appearances come to our mind. The example that is given is a playground. Say you have a huge playground, football field or someplace where different kinds of games are going on. It is all just play and there is a huge space in which things can happen. But similar to games going on, it is not anything to be terribly concerned about. Likewise, the Natural Mind is that space, that environment, in which all different kinds of appearances, good or bad, can arise, just like that playground. The advice is to not to be too concerned, too worried, too involved or grasping at whatever appearances arise. Sometimes when a person feels happy they really grasp or cling onto the experience very tightly. For example, if they won millions of dollars in the lottery, they would be overjoyed and feeling very good. On the other hand, if things go wrong, some misfortune to yourself or a family member, or a business going bad, and you cling very tightly to that, you will get extremely despondent. The advice here is not to worry so much about or cling to it, and to not assign reality to whatever appearances arise. This is a really good view for us to keep in mind in our daily life. When different feelings, pleasant or unpleasant arise, simply realize it is all within the playground of intrinsic awareness and Natural Mind. Do not be too concerned about what appears.

15. Dakini Tog-beb Ma

No. 15 Dakini Tog-beb Ma

The Dakini Tog-beb Ma of (Tibetan) Menyag ancestry showed the Dakini Namkha Cham of Uddiyana

Sign number 15: inviting light from the sphere of Awareness .

Meaning 15: Natural Mind is beyond grasped objects. Not abiding in perceptions, it pervades all of existence. Since, ultimately, there are no names, a name for wisdom does not exist. Since it cannot be shown in a conventional way, and is without production and disintegration, it is like the indestructible Yung Drung diamond.

Thus she spoke.

The main thrust of this has already been stated. Natural Mind is beyond any object of dualistic thought. Many names are given to the Natural Mind—transcendent wisdom, self-arising wisdom, self-knowing wisdom—but in the end, all of those are just names, just labels. From the point of view of it not really being what those names indicate, it is beyond dualistic thought. The source is inexpressible, there is no name for it. Labels cannot reveal the true nature. From the aspect of it not expanding or diminishing, it is compared to the indestructible diamond swastika.

16. Dakini Namkha Cham

No. 16 Dakini Namkha Cham

The Dakini Namkha Cham of Uddiyana showed the Shiwer Dakini Ötang Ma

Sign number 16: gathering five drops.

Meaning 16: The mind of Pure Awareness cannot be revealed as, 'This is it.' There is nothing that can measure or symbolize Yung-Drung-Mind. Natural Mind is primordially free from gathering and dispersing. I bow to Dharmakaya in which appearances are self-liberated.

Thus she spoke.

We can get some idea of the meaning of Natural Mind by hearing the teachings and by reading scriptures, but not precisely. We cannot really understand exactly what it is this way. The understanding has to come through the experience of our own practice. This indicates that learning and gaining experience through practice should accompany each other. It 'cannot be revealed as, this is it,' means you can get an idea, but it cannot be completely explained because it is beyond words.

Saying it is beyond words does not mean it is beyond experience. This is something that you can experience through your meditation and practice. It is principally through your own experience that you can identify or recognize it. Natural Mind can be spoken of in terms of examples and metaphors like light, space, the ocean, or the sun, but those are just approximations.

Being 'primordially free from gathering and dispersing,' means that the base and appearances are inseparable. Think of Natural Mind as being like the basis, and appearances as being the energy and manifestation from that basis. In fact, they are never separate. Appearances being released into Dharmakaya, Bonku, is natural. It is the natural state of things. It is also how we experience appearances in practice, as being liberated into the Dharmakaya.

17. Dakini Ötang Ma

No. 17 Dakini Ötang Ma

The Shiwer Dakini Ötang Ma showed the Kashmiri Dakini Gyan-den Ma

Sign number 17: pressing the body with ten fingers.

Meaning 17: Since Yung Drung Natural Mind spreads everywhere, from center to outermost edges, it is great space. Since it is ultimately immutable, it is indestructible great space. Since it is free of contrivances of acceptance and rejection, it is unimaginable great space. Since it is never exhausted however you use it, is very precious great space.

Thus she spoke.

The metaphor of the sky, the example of space, is very revealing. It does not illustrate just one facet or characteristic of Natural Mind, but many. Just as space does not have a center or edges, likewise Natural Mind pervades everywhere and does not have any center, border or edges. Natural Mind is unchanging like space. Just like no matter whether it is sunny or raining, however the weather changes, the space in which it happens does not change. Similarly, Natural Mind is immutable.

Everyone has experiences of happiness and sadness, but these are just changes in the way things appear to us; Natural Mind itself is unchanging. There is no effort that can change space. It cannot be rejected, denied or proven. Just like space is free from effort, Natural Mind is free from effort. Just like space is inexhaustible no matter how much you use it, likewise Natural Mind is inexhaustible. With this one example of space, we can find a lot of characteristics symbolizing Natural Mind.

18. Dakini Gyan-den Ma

No. 18 Dakini Gyan-den Ma

The Kashmiri Dakini Gyan-den Ma showed the Gyer Dakini Drag-chen Tsal

Sign number 18: directly pulling with meditative equipoise.

Meaning 18: Since Natural Mind, directionless space, has never rejected anything, delusions and karma, like clouds and mist, arise and dissolve. Whatever is grasped within Pure Awareness never passes outside of Natural Mind. All of existence appears and is released within Natural Mind. Since positive and negative are undifferentiated, there is no dividing of Natural Mind. Since it is never clarified or obscured, it is wide open day and night.

Thus she spoke.

Both transcendent wisdom and delusions arise from the basis of Natural State. Similar to clouds and mists arising in space, they arise due to certain causes and conditions. We do not speak about Natural Mind getting transcendent wisdom or getting rid of delusions. Whatever arises from Natural Mind, whether it is transcendent wisdom or delusion, does not leave, surpass or go out of Natural Mind. This means giving up grasping at positive things, such as something one wants or needs. And, likewise, giving up grasping of negative things as something I have to get rid of or abandon. This release or liberation of grasping into the Natural State is like becoming childlike, not holding onto things or grasping at things tightly. Discrimination derived from grasping diminishes; for example, one is not so attached to friends or enemies, to my side versus their side. This is a sign of grasping being liberated into

Natural Mind that is experienced by practitioners who become absorbed in their practice. When there becomes no difference between day and night, their practice proceeds all the time. When there is no difference between day and night, that is a sign of meditation having occurred.

19. Dakini Drag-chen Tsal

No. 19 Dakini Drag-chen Tsal

The Gyer Dakini Drag-chen Tsal showed Dakini Namkha Nyima Öden Ma

Sign number 19: pressing her palms to her waist on each side.

Meaning 19: Since Natural Mind is immeasurable, it is primordially dimensionless. Since Dharmakaya is spontaneously existent, discrimination of good and bad is self-liberated. Since faults are destroyed from the base, good qualities are naturally complete. Since the King of Awareness is realized, delusions are already annihilated.

Thus she spoke.

Most of the meaning here has been concealed. The last line, "Since the King of Awareness is realized, delusions are already annihilated" is similar to when in the midst of war and the opposing king is captured, then the entire opposing army is brought under control. If you understand the base and appearances as being inseparable, then there is no need to be afraid of delusions or conflicted states of mind arising. This can help you to deal with the stresses and worries that come up in your daily life. Likewise with frightening experiences or appearances in the bardo, the intermediate state after death, they can be well dealt with through this method and anything fearful can be released. Without understanding that connection between the basis and the appearances as Natural Mind's manifestations, if you try to apply other antidotes to those different frightening or disturbing thoughts and delusions, there could be benefit, but it will not get down to the main point. Going back to the example of waging war, applying other antidotes would be like capturing some of the other army's soldiers, but you do not win the war that way. This shows, mainly, that we need to understand that whatever experiences of samsara or nirvana arise, they are manifestations of the Natural Mind.

20. Dakini Namkha Nyima Öden Ma

No. 20 Dakini Namkha Nyima Öden Ma

Dakini Namkha Nyima Öden Ma showed Dakini Nyima Tong-Kyab Ma

Sign number 20: the sign of a heart, like three magical mirrors.

Meaning 20: Since space is unrestricted, don't tether it with dualistic grasping.

If you cannot be unreactive to dualistic appearances, the sun of wisdom will set.

If thought does not arise as Natural Mind, you will try to climb the paths and stages but wisdom will disappear. If you do not befriend the demon of negative emotions your path of practice will become impassable.

Thus she spoke.

In general, to talk about this particular subject would require an extensive explanation. As you meditate, if you cling to the idea of the emptiness being empty, that is not correct. In other words, if you grasp onto the concept that it needs to be empty, that is not the correct approach. The main thing is that grasping needs to disintegrate. You need to settle the mind without perception of subject or object, without objectifying object and subject. It is beyond objectifying either the subject or object.

There is no thought process that involves gradually improving the ordinary mind. For instance, we discussed samadhi and how it is used as a mental factor for improving meditation. This kind of procedure is not involved here. If you apply this kind of method to try to the improve ordinary mind, it will cause the primordial wisdom to set or wane.

As you meditate, there will be forms that appear to your sight or sounds that resound in your hearing, but by not paying attention to them we settle into Natural Mind. It is not a matter of tightening your concentration or needing more intensity in your meditation. It is more a matter of your awareness being relaxed into the Natural State. When unpleasant feelings or experiences arise, it is a matter of letting go of them and relaxing into meditation. When you let go of clinging to appearances and delusions, then you let go into that emptiness view. That is conducive for approaching the emptiness aspect. You can also settle into the factor of appearances. Those appearances are the appearing factor naturally arising. When those appearances are allowed to arise in emptiness, that is the practice. When those sounds or sights arise in meditation, do not follow them or try to stop them. Whatever good or bad things appear, you need to be able to release them all. The example is that of a courtyard or playground where all practice takes place. When you let go of good or bad appearances, this is the practice. This is how the meditation evolves. When you become completely absorbed in it, then it proceeds regardless of whether it is day or night.

21. Dakini Nyima Tong-Kyab Ma

No. 21 Dakini Nyima Tong-Kyab Ma

Dakini Nyima Tong-Kyab Ma showed Dakini Maha Sukasiddhi

Sign number 21: Sign of Pure Awareness's own radiance; pressing down on the body.

Meaning 21: If you don't hold the meaning with confidence the daughter of effort will run wild. If you don't accept protection from the guardian of the view, the dear son, your own mind, will be destroyed like an enemy. If you don't post the sentry of meditation, being known as a great yogi will be meaningless. If you don't tame the wild elephant of conduct, your view will become that of an ordinary person.

Thus she spoke.

There are many examples given here for the meaning. This primarily means that we need to develop confidence in regard to our view, our meditation and our conduct. We want our view to be objectless. If we do not meditate in the objectless state, we will not be able to get control of our mind. Because ordinary mind constantly gets involved in many various objects and is constantly changing like the weather, it is not stable. We cannot trust the ordinary mind too much because it is constantly changing. You cannot get the mind to sign on the dotted line. For example, when we sign a contract with someone we are saying that this is my promise. You cannot get anything like that from the ordinary mind. Therefore, we need to meditate without objects. Natural Mind is immutable and is not affected by causes and conditions.

In terms of meditation, we can be free from wandering, free

from distraction. Like the saying, "Meditate, meditate, don't meditate." The meaning of meditation is being undistracted. If you cannot proceed without distraction, your meditation will not develop or progress.

Conduct is liberated into the great space of emptiness. We speak of the conduct on this spiritual path as being free from adopting or abandoning, free from holding or rejecting. Being without grasping in conduct, for example, is similar to not caring much about whether you are wearing very fancy clothes or wearing something disheveled. Or, for example, of not caring much about whether you are wearing your hair in dreadlocks or shaving it off. Not caring about that kind of thing, not adding any concepts about it, is similar to that idea of conduct. If you are very attached in your conduct, saying I need to wear certain clothes or a certain color and do certain things, then your conduct becomes just like an ordinary person. If you do not tame the wild elephant of conduct, your conduct is just like that of an ordinary person. When an elephant acts wildly and jumps into the water and all the water spills out, or runs into bushes or trees or into a house and knocks them down, the wild elephant destroys all that it encounters. This is a brief explanation of the view, meditation, and action of the spiritual path.

22. Dakini Maha Sukasiddhi

No. 22 Dakini Maha Sukasiddhi

The Dakini Maha Sukasiddhi showed the Cho family Dakini Bon-chig

Sign number 22: the sign of clear meaning, hands joined.

Meaning 22: Since Natural Mind has no past or future, it is connected to all Buddhas of the three times. Since Natural Mind includes immeasurable compassion, it is connected to all sentient beings. Realizing it is the place of all arising, abiding, and dissolving, it is connected with all paths and results. Since Emptiness and appearances are liberated in Pure Awareness, the fruit is attained without effort.

Thus she spoke.

There is no dividing up Natural Mind into time. In terms of a person, we can speak of a time line. For instance, there is a particular time when a person attains enlightenment. In Natural Mind, past, present and future Buddhas are all mixed because at any time it is one, a singularity. Immeasurable compassion is encompassed within Natural Mind, therefore it is connected to all sentient beings of the three realms. Compassion is a natural manifestation or energy of Natural Mind. It is immeasurable compassion, one of the Four Immeasurables, that pervades all living beings. That is why the most powerful prayer for us to say is the aspiration that all living beings abide in Natural Mind. The ultimate point of release in Natural Mind makes the path and result always together. It is not like there is some other result that needs to be obtained.

23. Dakini Bon-chig

No. 23 Dakini Bon-chig

The Cho family Dakini Bon-chig showed

Sign number 23: collecting the life-essence of the Gurus.

Meaning 23: Since it is not born from causes and conditions, there is no basis for an original production. Since it abides in the great unknown, in the middle there is no place of abiding. Since Dharmakaya is immutable there is no way for it to end. Since existence is liberated in the ultimate sphere of Pure Awareness there are no resultant three Bodies that were sought to be attained.

Thus she spoke.

Most of the meaning of this has already been explained. The first part states that Natural Mind is not generated from causes or secondary causes. It is primordially free from any basis of birth. As for where it abides, there is not much you can say except that it is abiding in itself. That is one subject that is likely to cause debate or issue. The question would be something like "Where does the sky stay?" "Does the sky stay in the sky?" It is immutable, unchanging, and there is no saying where it finally goes. It is not produced, does not abide anywhere, and finally does not go anywhere. Usually, in terms of different paths or vehicles, a result is something that is aspired to or something to be attained in the future. Here because all appearances and phenomena have already been released in Natural Mind, it is only a matter of remembering it. This is speaking about the source of production, abiding and dissolving.

24. Dakini Bon-chig

No. 24 Dakini Bon-chig

Sign number 24 is the White AH Mind Transference.

Meaning 24: In Self-Originated Wisdom there is no reliance upon paths and stages to be attained. Since it does not rely upon cause and effect, it is a radiance that pervades space. It is not interrupted by conditions, nor destroyed by antidotes. Since Pure Awareness is self-liberated, the result is free of production and destruction.

Thus she spoke.

When the body of self-arisen primordial wisdom manifests, reliance upon the gradual path is utterly exhausted. This kind of statement, often found in Dzogchen scriptures, states that without practicing the gradual path, the result is quickly obtained. What this is saying is that there is no gradual path or graduated stages. It is a maintaining of meditation, a constant meditation, where all existence and appearances are immediately liberated into Natural Mind. This way, the Natural Mind is self-liberated, self-released. There is no change in the basis, there is no change in the result; both are unchanging. In other vehicles, the basis and the result are different; here, the basis and result are the same.

25. Dakini Bon-chig

No. 25 Dakini Bon-chig

Sign number 25 is Guru Yoga at the crown.

Meaning 25: This self-originated Wisdom Awareness has never been produced or destroyed by causes and conditions. There is no enumeration of paths, stages, and results. It is free of being an object of the seventeen concepts.

Thus she spoke.

There are no paths and stages like there are in other practices. For instance, in the sutra presentation, there are five paths or ten stages, each with its own particular result. When you get the result of one path, you move on to the next higher path, and get the result of that. Here the result is one and there is no progressively higher result. Therefore, there are no stages of the path. There is a mention of seventeen visions, meaning seventeen concepts. There is, indeed, one categorization into seventeen, but in general, thoughts are innumerable. We have twenty-one thousand thoughts in the course of a single day. No matter how many there are, they are easily liberated in Natural Mind. If it troubles you to think that there are twenty-one thousand thoughts, you can think there are a few thoughts. Do not be disturbed. You don't have to worry about that too much!

26. Dakini Bon-chig

No. 26 Dakini Bon-chig

Sign number 26 is six self-clear, turning wheels.

Meaning 26: Since a thunderbolt of Awareness Arises from Emptiness, causes of attainment are self-liberated. Since a thunderbolt of Awareness Transcending Cause and Effect arises, sequential paths (yana-vehicles) are self-liberated. Since a thunderbolt of Awareness Transcending the Faulty arises, grasping is self-liberated. Since a thunderbolt of Awareness of Emptiness and Appearances arises, a fabricator is self-liberated.

Thus she spoke.

This meditation is referred to as the liberated path, the path of release. In the other vehicles, the procedure presented is that there is a path of abandoning delusions, and that is then followed by a path of release. There is a particular illusion or ignorance that is abandoned by the meditative path which is then followed by the path of release—that of having been liberated. Here, however, there is no perception of faults that need to be abandoned. They are not regarded as negative. They are simply released or liberated.

Whatever happens in the course of our day, whether pleasant or unpleasant, happiness, or sadness, that is the entire environment for our practice. Recognize that thoughts arise and release them. The ability to release upon recognition is similar to meeting a friend that you have not seen in many years, and instantly you recognize them. This is similar to the instantaneous release of appearances and thoughts. This release upon recognition, happening automatically and very naturally, is similar to a snake untying its own knots. This release of positive or negative thoughts, pleasant and unpleasant feelings—releasing them upon recognition—is like the thief coming into an empty house and realizing that there is nothing there to steal.

With respect to Intrinsic Awareness striking like a thunderbolt, sometimes people have a sudden understanding of Natural Mind. There is an account in the teachings of two people in ancient times receiving the teachings: one had always acted honorably and had practiced Dharma but had never received the Dzogchen teachings; the another had not been a practitioner at all and had done a lot of bad things, such as creating negative karma. They both came to receive the Dzogchen teachings at the same time. It is said that there is no certainty that the one who had been a practitioner before would realize and understand any faster than the one who had not. Sometimes it is just realized like a thunderbolt.

Different philosophies that are studied throughout the ten different systems are all instantly released. There is no grasping at something being good or bad; grasping is instantly released. Since all phenomena and emptiness arise in Natural Mind suddenly, like a thunderbolt, the creator self-liberates into its own nature. By understanding that the basis of emptiness is one with phenomena or appearances that arise from it, they are both liberated.

27. Dakini Bon-chig

No. 27 Dakini Bon-chig

The one who manifests those creations or appearances is released in the Natural Mind.

Sign number 27 is pointing out Natural Mind with an illuminating mirror.

Meaning 27: Natural Mind is unborn, beyond the way of words, whether simply or elaborately spoken; and beyond the four dualistic conventionalities: existing, seeing, appearing, or being conventionally accepted reality; this is the perspective of Dzogchen.

Thus she spoke.

Natural Mind is beyond birth and death. It is unborn and undying. It is also beyond embellishing or simplifying. Whether the Natural Mind is explained very extensively or very briefly, either way, it cannot really be described. However, what is experienced in meditation can be partially described to a certain extent. If it weren't possible, it would be impossible to introduce the subject or teach it to anyone. Describing it and explaining it is just using symbols and articulating sounds to induce some level of understanding in a person. Such is the case with the word Dzogchen. We have those two syllables, *Dzog* and *chen*. The first of these syllables, *Dzog*, means perfected or complete. It means that all existence and appearances are completely included in or completely perfected in Natural Mind. Another example of an aspect of completeness is that all the elements are included within space. Similarly, the capacities of the four elements are also included in Natural Mind. The example of the elements is something that is more apparent to us, easier for us to understand, since all the elements are included in space.

Natural Mind is not as obvious or easy for the mind to perceive, but the elements can help us to understand. Because Natural Mind is empty, it encompasses all appearances, just like space encompasses all the elements. Because it is the source of both Samsara and Nirvana, it is compared to the ground, from which all different flowers and forests grow. Because Natural Mind has the capacity to release all negativity, faults, karma and so on, it is like the capacity of water to wash away dirt. Because Natural Mind has the ability to destroy clinging and grasping, it has the capacity of the wind to blow things away. It is like fire, being able to burn away all grasping at the identities of things.

The qualities of the Six Perfections are included within the meaning of the first syllable, *Dzog*. All these are complete within Natural Mind. For instance, the perfection of generosity is characterized as being a lack of attachment, a lack of clinging. Since in the base of Natural Mind there is no attachment, no clinging, the perfection of giving is complete within it.

Because it is beyond any effortful morality of abandoning faults or contamination, the perfection of ethical discipline is also complete in Natural Mind. It is said to be a primordial morality of ethical discipline that is and has been kept without beginning or end. It is called the ethical discipline that does not need to be guarded. It is free of grasping anything to be abandoned or to be adopted. It is said to be the guarding of morality that is not guarding. From that point of view, of being free of effortful perseverance, it is neither too relaxed nor too tight.

In speaking about the perfection of patience, there is nothing to be feared in Natural Mind. Patience or forbearance has, as one of its most important significances, the patience to realize and understand Natural Mind. In some of the lower vehicles, when they look at the procedure or the mode of description of Dzogchen, some say that it is not right, that there is something wrong about it, that one has to meditate on a deity or mantra. Here, in the path of Dzogchen, it is not said that you cannot meditate on deities or recite mantras, but it is asserted that it is not absolutely necessary. Practitioners of the lower vehicles say "no, that is not right. One could not maintain patience." One kind of patience upon hearing the assertions of Dzogchen would be to say, "Okay, maybe I do not know everything. Maybe there could be some accuracy in that." If you can meditate with patience and conduct yourself in accordance with the conduct of Dzogchen, great benefit can be derived. If you are not afraid of it, if you do not criticize it, that is a sign of patience. As far as patience being included in the Natural Mind of Dzogchen, there is nothing to be afraid of in Natural Mind. There is no place for anxiety or narrow mindedness in Natural Mind. From that point of view, patience is complete within it.

In maintaining your Dzogchen meditation, if you do not come under the power of thoughts, then perseverance is complete. The perfection of concentration is complete within it; the Natural Mind is sustained continuously. There is no setting of the mind within it, nor is there a letting go of it. Natural Mind has its own sustainability. There is no intent to apply it or to let go of it. It sustains itself.

Finally, the perfection of wisdom is complete in Natural Mind in that it knows itself and it is the absence of subject-object duality. Thus, the qualities that are included or complete in Dzogchen are infinite. As you maintain the emptiness aspect and the appearance aspect of Natural Mind, all these infinite qualities are included in it.

The second part of the word Dzogchen, *chen*, means great. It means that there is no practice superior to it. There are many ways in which it is the greatest. It is great because it is the swiftest path to realization. It is great because it is not understandable by the vehicles that are lower than it. It is great from the point of view of it being so extremely profound.

28. Dakini Bon-chig

No. 28 Dakini Bon-chig

Sign number 28 is offering the body in a feast-gathering (tsog-ganachakra).

Meaning 28: Self-liberated, Natural Mind is the essence of the meaning of Emptiness. Views asserting singularity (partisanship) or multiplicity are a pitfall. Beyond all hope and fear, beyond effort, Natural Mind is a vast vessel of great bliss.

Thus she spoke.

This is the body offered as a feast or tsok-ganachakra. In general, the body is empty and is an empty form. If you know well how the body is released in Natural Mind, then that is what is meant as the body being of empty form. Because the body is an empty form, anything can be done with it. What the Dakini is doing here, offering up her body as a feast, is similar to the practice of cutting called *Chöd*, where the body is offered up. With the understanding of the body being empty, there is no attachment to it. One gets to the point of abandoning expectations and fears. Emptiness is like an infinite vessel within which everything can be placed; not bound by clinging to hopes and fears, not bound by effortful thinking or by persevering with ordinary mind.

When we talk about the sky being empty, that is a gross understanding of emptiness. A being who thinks all phenomena is like space takes birth in one of the four levels of the formless realm because they cling to that idea. Or they may become trapped in the formless realm of samsara because they think everything is empty and their meditation is like space. But that is a perception that is bound by ignorance; it is a clinging to the conception that things are like space. Because they have sustained a focus on phenomena being like space, it becomes more and more concrete for them. It becomes more fixed within their mind.

There are likewise four successively subtler levels of the formless realm: infinite space, infinite consciousness, nothing at all, and neither existence nor non-existence. Each of these becomes more and more subtle, but each one of them is bound by clinging. There is a latching on to things that are qualities of Natural Mind, the inability to let go of them.

When we rest our mind in an uncontrived, unfabricated state, we need to go beyond and transcend all of those concepts. Holding biased views and drawing parallels is an error. That is what is meant here. If we latch onto one of these qualities in this way, if we concretize and reify it, then that is an error. It is a mistake. This is why it is important for us to understand some of the subtleties of meditation. There are many different kinds of meditation and many different levels of meditation. We need to understand these distinctions and not concoct a unification of something. We need to be able to transcend all of those similar kinds of ideas.

'Natural Mind is a vast vessel of great bliss" refers to Natural Mind being a vast vessel that holds everything. The fact that living beings experience happiness is a sign of Natural Mind being present. The ability of our eyes to perceive forms, the ability of our mind to cognize things, the ability to undertake and accomplish vast activities with our mind, are all signs of the Natural Mind within us. That all appearances are included in Natural Mind is not just a verbal description. It is an actual fact of our lives, from birth to death. For example, one person can be someone's sibling, could also be someone's aunt or uncle, and could also be someone's niece or nephew. Similarly, Natural Mind can be the factor of emptiness, it can be the factor of appearances, it can be the factor of compassion. It can be a factor of all the different perfections, not to mention the sixty different permutations of the perfections. Similar to the example of the person who can be a number of different things in relation to different people, Natural Mind can be all of these things. It includes all of these. And it is not just that different labels are put on it, but it is that all these qualities are actually spontaneously present within it. Just because someone is someone's wife, does not mean that she is not someone's niece. Similarly, someone can be a father as well as a son. It is all happening simultaneously.

29. Dakini Bon-chig

No. 29 Dakini Bon-chig

Sign number 29 is the mudra of the lion released.

Meaning 29: Because Awareness is completely pure, even the name, samsara, does not exist. Without abandoning the five aggregates, enlightenment is primordially attained. All the ornaments illuminating Natural Mind are complete. Samantabhadra equanimity does not fall into partisanship.

Thus she spoke.

We can say that because transcendent wisdom is primordial, there has never been samsara, nor even the name samsara. How does samsara arise? It arises through ignorance and clinging to self. Samsara and nirvana cannot be beyond Natural Mind; they are within it. The process of how samsara takes place is similar to what happens when a bardo being takes birth in another body. First of all, at the time of death the body is discarded and Natural Mind manifests. Because the manifestations of Natural Mind never cease, when there is light that appears and shines, the mind perceives the light as though it is coming from outside, from somewhere else. Then, through grasping, one conceives of inner and outer, subject and object. When the visual consciousness perceives an object, there are two sides that have been set up. The continuum of that gets grosser and grosser. One thought supports the next. It is just like water solidifying into ice in the winter. The concepts get grosser and grosser. In regard to the bardo, there is a reference to sounds, lights and rays. The first subtle appearances that arise easily become grosser, manifesting in grosser forms. They start off as different colored lights—red, yellow, green, blue and white—

and, as it gets grosser, it evolves into grosser phenomena. The elements of fire, earth, wind, water, and space arise from that. This evolves into the world that people then experience. That is what we call samsara. Samsara's not there from the beginning, but it arises through this misperception, this misconception.

Without abandoning the five aggregates, primordial Buddhahood is realized. There is no need to get rid of the aggregates. One point of clarification regarding the experience of lights arising from the Natural State in the bardo: perceiving it as coming from outside is the beginning of conceptuality. It is the beginning of the division into subject and object duality that evolves into samsara. The fact of the matter is, those lights do not come from outside. That is the mistake that is made. Realize this. Those appearances come from Natural Mind. It is when you do not realize that those appearances are Natural Mind manifesting, that the problems begin. Natural Mind encompasses everything equally without samsara being bad and nirvana being good, and so on. Without falling into partiality, it does not fall into the extremes of samsara or nirvana, and no matter how bad things are or how good things are, they do not effect or harm Natural Mind.

30. Dakini Bon-chig

No. 30 Dakini Bon-chig

Sign number 30 is the sign of being shielded by the Lord's command.

Meaning 30: Those who don't abide in this, who lack the fortune for it, are like someone who wants yogurt trying to milk a horn, or a dog trying to lick at space. This is a place of raksha-cannibals where the brightness of the elements has faded. By mixing nectar with poison you cut short the lives of living beings. By mixing-up view, meditation, conduct, and fruition you enter a pit of darkness. Degeneration of samaya will make heart's-blood pour from your mouth.

Thus she spoke.

This is from the point of view of this being a very profound instruction. If you receive these instructions, you really do not need other instructions. What this is particularly talking about is if somebody receives these teachings and does not respect them. We have discussed the view, meditation, conduct and results. We should maintain respect and reverence for these. This view is without object; it is objectless. If someone said not having any object for your meditation is a mistake, it is wrong and then this kind of problem will result. Here the teaching is that meditation is to be undistracted. If you disagree, and you say that is not correct, meditation is not non-distraction, a problem will result. This scripture is presented in the sense of being the final word. It is the final instruction. There is nothing beyond this. Within the structure of the nine vehicles, this is the ninth and highest vehicle. There is nothing that is beyond it, nothing that surpasses it. You can explain it in different ways but there is nothing that goes beyond it.

Questions and Answers

Question: When does a Dakini know when she's a Dakini. How does that process happen?

Answer: First of all, in terms of Dzogchen teachings, we can talk about beings that are ordinary and beings that are extraordinary. We would say that the ordinary person who has been introduced to Natural Mind is no longer ordinary. Now they are extraordinary, they are special. Once they are introduced to Natural Mind then they are special or exalted over an ordinary state. Grossly speaking, from that point on we can talk about three different stages of meditative experience. The first stage is sitting in sessions of meditation. The practitioners sit down on their meditation cushion and they recognize Natural Mind, but not otherwise.

In the second stage, there is never a separation between meditation and no meditation. Everything becomes meditation. Automatic or naturally arising meditation is the second stage. There is no longer a loss of awareness between meditation sessions.

The third level is a highly realized state in which one actually realizes that all phenomena are manifestations of transcendent awareness or Natural Mind. It is said that at this point you become a Dakini. I think that upon reaching the second level where there is not a lot of difference between meditation and out of meditation, you can pretty much say you are a Dakini at that point. It is hard to give an answer to that. It's a good question.

Question: Does the rainbow body occur spontaneously

when you realize all phenomena arise out of the natural state?

Answer: It does not necessarily mean that you attain a rainbow body. But generally, reaching the realization that all phenomena are a manifestation of the energy created by Natural Mind would be the point of being able to attain rainbow body and the culmination of realization.

Question: Are there signs when a practitioner is getting close to achieving rainbow body? Are there things that would appear in their life?

Answer: If you are talking about being close to attaining rainbow body, this would pertain to someone approaching death. To say what kinds of signs would arise would be difficult. Some practitioners, as they approach realization, become more and more childlike because they are letting go of holding onto so many things, grasping things. That may be considered a sign of someone getting closer to full enlightenment.

Question: Sometimes getting old and more childlike is not a positive thing.

Answer: It could be a factor of aging, especially if that is something that is just happening and they have not been practicing. If it happens as a result of the kinds of realizations that occur due to practice, then it is a sign of such realization.

Question: When you are in that natural state, how does it relate to the Sanskrit word samadhi?

Answer: The word samadhi, in Tibetan *ting-nge-dzin*, can be applied to a wide range of meditations. In regard to any kind of meditation in which you become absorbed, Natural Mind could be spoken of as a kind of samadhi. In Natural Mind meditation, we are actually beyond samadhi. The general presentation of samadhi from the teachings in logic and dialectics is a more ordinary kind of mind. It is talking about a consciousness that is focusing directly on something. Ordinarily, samadhi is used to describe a mind focused single-pointedly on an object; not wandering away from it or going anywhere else, but remaining or resting single-pointedly on an object. The presentation of calm abiding meditation, mental quiescence meditation, creates a sense of blessing or special experience. The mind is able to rest single-pointedly on an object through the force of samadhi, through the force of meditative absorption. That particular samadhi is identified as being a mental factor, just one factor or part of the mind. It is something that assists or enables the mind to remain single-pointedly focused on its object. As such, it is a mental factor. It is the factor that enables the mind to stay single-pointedly focused on its object. By developing and improving the practice of samadhi, the main mind can improve and at some point focus and realize its object. Then you can have meditative experience. As a result, a pliancy of the body and the mind can be attained.

Question: In the second phase of meditation practice you describe, after somebody has already begun to recognize their Natural Mind and it becomes more continuous or natural in the post-meditation state as well, would that be considered to be something like a Dzogchen or Mahamudra samadhi? If not, how you would describe that?

Answer: The word samadhi would not be used in that context. It is just a matter of whether you are able to rest in Natural Mind. Once you have opened the door to Natural Mind, it is as if this space has opened up, or like a light has been turned on. You rest in that, and it may be just for short periods at first. Then, when you can remain in that awareness all the time, you are in the second stage. As for this talk, the terms for ordinary mind and mental factors such as samadhi are not mixed. A good example is the sky clear of clouds.

Question: Basically, are you saying that as you meditate, whatever you experience as an element, emotion or a thought, we allow that to be there, and with our allowing it to be there, it dissolves into the Natural Mind.

Answer: Yes, correct.

Question: Do you have any suggestions for while we are meditating, we get sleepy or our focus starts to waiver, and we are unable to rest naturally?

Answer: Sometimes the mind might become agitated and it is difficult for us to rest in the natural state. There are modes of conduct that can be employed for that situation. It could be good to go into another place that is a little bit darker, not extremely bright or lit, or maybe to cool down a little bit. If the mind is too excited, you can take off clothing, put on the air-conditioning, and maybe eat a little bit larger meal. On the other hand, if the mind is becoming dull or sleepy, then the advice is the opposite. You can go to a high place where it is brightly lit, for example the upper story in the house that has more light.

Sometimes looking up into the sky can help, looking up into space. If it is a problem of too much excitement or agitation in the mind, it can be helpful to cast your gaze in a downward direction. If you are hitting a wall in your meditation, then you should not push it. Sometimes it is recommended to take a little break. If you are having difficulty and you push too hard, then it can create an attitude of when you think of meditation, it makes you sad and you don't look forward to it.

Question: What is the Dzogchen perspective on when you have a dream and then it comes true in your life?

Answer: The explanation from the point of view of Dzogchen would be that all realized qualities are spontaneously present in Natural Mind, which includes knowledge of the future and clairvoyance. It is natural that those kinds of qualities could emerge, such as knowledge of a future event.

Last night I had a dream. I was rushing to the bus stop with a friend and I had the ticket, but I did not know what time it was. When we got to the bus, I was carrying my bag and my friend was not helping. Then I realized that my friend is very good, and would not be like that. So then I realized that I must be dreaming. And I went on to practice dream yoga.

Question: I have a question about a type of recurring dream that shows up for me. It relates to waves that are described in the formless states. Not infrequently, I have dreams of space moving through itself, almost like fields of rippling light. It feels like a sort of energy. I met the Karmapa a number of years ago, and often when I have these dreams I see him. Sometimes there are aspects to the dream and sometimes there is a kind of formless state. I also often drop into these formless states while in normal consciousness. Thinking of it now, I can go partially into it. I see how this may be what you described as reification. What is the antidote to reification?

Answer: As the saying goes, "Meditate, meditate, don't meditate." Non-meditation is the supreme meditation. When there is an experience of vast or infinite space or consciousness like that, and the thought arises, "Oh, that's space or that's consciousness," then a subject-object duality has been set up. The person says, "Oh there is that." There is an observer of it and there is an object observed. When you have meditative equipoise, Natural Mind Dzogchen, that duality is not present. It is just one experience. There is no separation between the observed object and the observer. It is just a singularity of the sun rising. Whenever duality emerges from the labeling of an object by a subject, then that is not Dzogchen meditation of Natural Mind. The Tibetan word for remembering also means mindfulness. Mindfulness does have a place in meditation. It is a kind of checking, at times, to see if you are on track or not. Sometimes mindfulness can be present. For instance, if you lose the thread of your Dzogchen meditation, it is mindfulness to remember it and bring yourself back to that balance. That kind of mindfulness has a place. It is a useful function.

Question: When we are working with Natural Mind, we are working to recognize and also to let go. I want to ask about that. And when we are working with our dreams, lucid dreaming or realizing we are dreaming, what is our goal? Do we do some kind of practice?

Answer: The first part of what you said, about recognizing and letting go, that is accurate. The idea of letting go of grasping and clinging definitely has a place there. That is really the extent of what needs to be done in meditation.

As for the object of dream yoga, if you can be lucid in a dream, and ideally, if you can remember the Natural Mind and meditate, then that is enough. There is no need to do any other practice, visualization of deities and so forth. This is the same for the awakened state. If you do not lose your Natural Mind meditation in the course of working or walking, etc., then everything becomes practice. It is the same in a dream; if you can remember the natural state, that is best. Some practitioners and yogis will use dream yoga to do different daily meditations, like going to the Pure Land of Deities and Buddhas, but that is different.

Question: In Dzogchen, would it be helpful if one has the ability to develop the four formless absorptions and the four form absorptions, that are defined mostly in Theravadan teachings, but also mentioned in Mahayana? Would it be helpful to cultivate those, if one had the ability to do so, in Dzogchen?

Answer: I would say there is not much benefit to that in the context of Dzogchen meditation. But it may be useful for a beginner. The stages of shamata meditation are surpassed by meditations that combine shamata and vipassana. When it is purely shamata, they are lower, they are mundane. The meditations that combine the special insight of vipassana are supra-mundane, they go beyond that. In that process of shamatha meditation, more refined or subtler levels of mind are brought out. But they are only mundane, not transcendental, meditation. Dzogchen goes beyond that. In the process of shamatha meditation, there is ascension through realms of existence from grosser to more subtle. Looking at a lower level of existence is grosser. Dzogchen is more subtle. For instance, seeing forms in the form realm is like thinking "Oh, that's gross, I don't need that." Or "I don't want that." When in Dzogchen meditation, there is a simple release, a liberation of all forms into Natural Mind. There is not this kind of discrimination between "Oh, this is a grosser state and I don't want it; this is a more refined state that I want." That kind of discrimination is not present.

Question: I had some dreams where I realized that I was dreaming. It was like being the witness of the dream. When that happens, should I just relax into that? At that point, should I relax into that natural space?

Answer: First of all, it is important to be able to recognize that you are dreaming, to know that a dream is a dream. That is called lucid dreaming. If you can do that, the next step of remembering or recognizing the Natural Mind is very easy. If you can maintain the force of that Natural Mind understanding and realization, then you can go on with the dream. Actually, the hardest thing, first of all, is to wake up to the fact that you are dreaming. There are many different methods that can be applied to accomplish that first step.

Question: When you practice dream yoga, if you have got to get up and go to work later, can you totally relax and be fed by that experience, without worrying about not sleeping because you are meditating? Could you be in the natural state and eventually just get up and do your daily life, and not have to worry that you did not sleep as you were dreaming all night in the natural state?

Answer: If you are meditating in Natural Mind, you get even better rest than if you are just sleeping! You can also do both. You can get restful sleep and meditate in Natural Mind. You can set that intention as you go to sleep that you want to meditate in Natural Mind. If you set that motivation prior to going to sleep, that can lead to being able to be in meditation while you are sleeping. When you wake up, you can maintain the same continuum of the meditation; understand and keep a continuum from sleeping to the waking state. You have to develop quite a strong familiarity with meditation for that to happen. That is, what is what is meant by "there is no difference between day and night." It means that kind of meditation.

Question: What is the role of devotion and blessing?

Answer: A sign of having devotion and receiving blessings is when you can recognize Natural Mind and the practice helps you to dispel difficulties and suffering. That is the sign blessings are being received. You need to have reverence toward the teachings themselves. We speak about temporary reverence and devotion, and ultimate reverence and devotion. The temporary one is when the practice helps you alleviate and dispel problems and suffering in the course of your daily life. The ultimate one is one that can do the same for your migration through the bardo and into future lifetimes. There are many different types of teachings, such as the nine vehicles, for human beings with different faculties or capacities. Nine is kind of a rough description of many different levels.

The Dzogchen teachings' lineage traces back to Samantabhadra. Satrig Ersang, the Great Mother of Perfection of Wisdom is also the source—in the unveiling of herself, her emanating in various forms, as the dakini lineage, coming down to us. In the eighth century, it came down to the Tibetan Queen Choza Bonmo. Then in the eleventh century, it came in through this close lineage. There is also a lot to say about the long lineage.

Question: In some traditions, it is taught that in the bardo there can be very disturbing sounds and visions. So people are taught to use supports like visualizing a deity; for example, a wrathful deity. But in this tradition, we do not use any of that, we just rest in the natural state of the mind's perfection. We continually bring everything to the Natural State. Can we travel through the bardo without losing that Natural Mind?

Answer: Yes. It is similar to dreams, where sometimes you might have nightmares. So it all comes down to what we say in the prayer, "Please bless me to realize that all appearances are a form of Natural Mind itself." Likewise, our body is empty of form. It is a kind of practice that can be applied in dreams and in the bardo as well. Understand that the body is an empty form and use it as such. Then no problems are encountered.

Question: Something in your talk caught my attention. If you mix dutsi with poison, my mind is thinking the dutsi would override the poison because it is so powerful. But I think you said that the poison would diminish the dutsi. Is that correct?

Answer: You are talking about the problems that arise from polluting the instructions. We have really created a tremendous amount of wonderful, positive energy through attending to this subject, understanding Natural Mind in our practice and discussing these things. We need to dedicate this positive energy not just for ourselves but for the sake of all beings' happiness, that they should be able to meet with these instructions and free themselves from suffering. We can also dedicate the merit for the pacification of problems in the environment, for world peace, and especially for freedom from disturbance by the elements in our own particular area. Along with that, any particular challenges or problems that family member or friends or partners are meeting and dealing with can also be brought to mind, and you can make a specific dedication for them along with the general dedication. You can also remember those who have passed and dedicate energy for their well-being and a fortunate onward journey.

The Root Text

Holy Women of Great Perfection

Thirty Signs and Meanings of Ultimate Nature
in the Ancient Tibetan Tradition

*From the White Sky Primordial Mind-Essence
Clearance of Extremes: Cycle of Essential instructions
of the Male and Female Lineages*

Homage to the Principal Dakini of the Five Sets of Dakinis!

Great Mother Satrig Ersang emanated a beautiful samaya-dakini, Dzema Yiwongma, who taught these blessed instructions of the female lineage to the goddesses (*walmo*) and dakinis. All those of the female lineage were satisfied and cleared of doubts. The samaya-dakini Dzema Yiwongma plucked the written instructions in ink of lapis lazuli written on copper sheets from space, blessed it, and gave it to them. The Indian Dakini Ulishag translated them into Sanskrit. The meaning is presented in two aspects: direct demonstration of the non-verbal signs; and verbal explanation of all the meanings as being included within Natural Mind.

Samaya-Dakini Dzema Yiwongma gave the Indian dakini symbolic indication number 1: a rope of light in space.

Meaning 1: This primordially existent bodhicitta-dharmakaya lacks the five aggregates; it is beyond flourishing and declining, birth and death, joining and separating; it cannot be killed or destroyed. All existence is included within Natural Mind, primordially abiding within dharmakaya. From the mind-transmission vidhyadhara lineage, it was then passed on to the worldly deities.

Thus she spoke.

The Indian Dakini Ulishag revealed to Dakini Goddess Namkha Ökyi Gyelmo sign number 2: palms bursting forth in space.

Meaning 2. Because it is ultimately unending within the non-declining victory banner of Bodhicitta-Natural-Mind, Dharmakaya is without increase or decrease; it is changeless; it is the great indestructible yung-drung of the three times, a primordial victory banner that does not abandon the root basis of samsara and nirvana.

Thus she spoke.

Dakini Goddess Namkha Ökyi Gyelmo revealed to Dakini Salwa Yingchug Ma of Razhag sign number 3: Her body standing in space.

Meaning 3: The defining characteristic of Natural Mind is being primordially enlightened. That Yung-Drung-Bodhicitta is beyond thought, causes and conditions. Leaving body and mind unaltered, arise in the singular Dharmakaya, free from extremes of appearance and emptiness; the primordially self-arising body.

Thus she spoke.

Dakini Salwa Yingchug Ma of Razhag revealed to Dakini Ökyi

Lama of Zhangzhung sign number 4: pulling at the nape of her neck with her right hand fingers.

Meaning 4: Primordially unobscured, Natural Mind is empty and clear. By mind looking at mind, appearing objects are exhausted. Then, settle in a state beyond observed objects, with nothing to see. This is the empty space of the mind; objects of meditation are released within pristine awareness.

Thus she spoke.

Dakini Ökyi Lama of Zhangzhung showed the lady of the Dong family, Dakini Kharmokyong, sign number 5: the automatic stopping of thought.

Meaning 5: Space is an example for Natural Mind. The meaning exemplified is being primordially awakened. Emptiness and clarity, unconditioned, pure awareness pervades all from center to edges. Dharmakaya is empty, beyond inherently existent objects. Settle, integrating with pure awareness, on the basis of whatever appears.

Thus she spoke.

The Lady Dong, Dakini Kharmokyong, showed Dakini Mangje Salgye-ö of Persia sign number 6: light in space.

Meaning 6: When we examine Natural Mind, whatever appears is primordially pure. Since natural appearances are released, this is nondual dharmakaya. All of existence is liberated, not rejected; this is supreme awakening. Whatever happens in appearances is manifestation of Pure Awareness.

Thus she spoke.

Dakini Mang-je Salgye-ö of Persia showed the lower caste Dakini Dutsi-kyong of Uddiyana sign number 7: her arms embracing her thighs.

Meaning 7: In the space of Natural Mind, primordially empty, all-pervasive, arise its mudra manifestations, mandalas, forms and colors. They never move outside of the mind's ultimate nature. Not moving out of the mind's true nature is the seal of Natural Mind.

Thus she spoke.

Dakini Dutsi-kyong of Uddiyana showed the Indian Dakini Thuchen of Phamting the sign number 8: moving down and pressing with her hand.

Meaning 8: Since Natural Mind is not objectifiable, Dharmakaya is beyond effort. It has no color, no shape, no dimensions. Since it is primordially beyond production and disintegration it cannot be destroyed by anything. Abide in objectless spaciousness, empty and all-pervasive.

Thus she spoke.

The Indian Dakini Thuchen of Phamting showed the Chinese Dakini Selwa Ödrön sign number 9: transference of consciousness into a wrathful Deity.

Meaning 9: Since existence is the shining of pure luminosity that far exceeds the sun and moon, dwelling in all pervasive luminosity dispels the darkness of ignorance. Since it is primordially enlightened, samsara is completely uprooted. Since its previous and later qualities are not different, the three times are of one nature.

Thus she spoke.

The Chinese Dakini Selwa Ödrön showed the Dakini Drimé Dangden Ma of Yorpo the sign number 10: transference of consciousness into base-clear-light, Natural Mind.

Meaning 10: Natural Mind is the nature of great nectar. Since it enjoys everything within and without, whatever appears is nectar. Since it seals whatever appears, Natural Mind is the supreme of nectars. Since it pervades immeasurable space, Dharmakaya is nectar.

Thus she spoke.

Dakini Drimé Dangden Ma of Yorpo showed the Dakini of the Cho family, Ökyi Dzutrul Tön, sign number 11: right hand lifting the right knee.

Meaning 11: Natural Mind is like space; it is primordially empty, selfless, and all-pervasive. Natural Mind is like a lotus; it is free from extremes of good and bad, both outside and inside. Natural Mind is like a jewel treasure; whatever is wished or needed arises from it. Natural Mind is like a rainbow; it is the Dharmakaya of nondual appearance and emptiness.

Thus she spoke.

The Dakini of the Cho family, Ökyi Dzutrul Tön, showed the Dakini Dzutrul Natsog Tön of Drusha sign number 12: six wheels of light.

Meaning 12: Natural Mind lacks inherent existence and is free from the extreme of permanence. Since it is never missing, it is free from the extreme of nihilism. It does not cling to the six objects of consciousness, and is free from self-grasping. It is beyond color and directions, free from all clinging to inherent existence.

Thus she spoke.

The Dakini Dzutrul Natsog Tön of Drusha showed the Lung-gyen Dakini Nangwa Datön Ma sign number 13: a union of lights of method and wisdom.

Meaning 13: Within the Great Permanence of absence of meeting and parting, liberation and deception, there is spontaneously established Great Nihilism absent of ego grasping. Since existence is self-sealed, it is the Great Self. Since existence is true nature appearing, it is the Great Grasping of Reality.

Thus she spoke.

The Lung-gyen Dakini Nangwa Datön Ma showed the Dakini Tog-beb Ma of Menyag ancestry sign number 14: squatting like a dog or lion, gazing into space.

Meaning 14: Not rejecting appearances of light, they are recognized as manifestations of Pure Awareness. Any grasping conceptions that arise are the playground of Pure Awareness. Not thinking about what appears, it is Pure Awareness' place of liberation. Primordially not thinking of anything is the resultant Liberation.

Thus she spoke.

The Dakini Tog-beb Ma of (Tibetan) Menyag ancestry showed the Dakini Namkha Cham of Uddiyana sign number 15: inviting light from the sphere of Awareness.

Meaning 15: Natural Mind is beyond grasped objects. Not abiding in perceptions, it pervades all of existence. Since, ultimately, there are no names, a name for wisdom does not exist. Since it cannot be shown in a conventional way, and is without production and disintegration, it is like the indestructible Yung-Drung diamond.

Thus she spoke.

The Dakini Namkha Cham of Uddiyana showed the Shiwer Dakini Ötang Ma sign number 16: gathering five drops.

Meaning 16: The mind of Pure Awareness cannot be revealed as, 'This is it.' There is nothing that can measure or symbolize Yung-Drung-Mind. Natural Mind is primordially free from gathering and dispersing. I bow to Dharmakaya in which appearances are self-liberated.

Thus she spoke.

The Shiwer Dakini Ötang Ma showed the Kashmiri Dakini Gyan-den Ma sign number 17: pressing the body with ten fingers.

Meaning 17: Since Yung-Drung Natural Mind spreads everywhere, from center to outermost edges, it is great space. Since it is ultimately immutable, it is indestructible great space. Since it is free of contrivances of acceptance and rejection, it is unimaginable great space. Since it is never exhausted however you use it, is very precious great space.

Thus she spoke.

The Kashmiri Dakini Gyan-den Ma showed the Gyer Dakini Drag-chen Tsal sign number 18: directly pulling with meditative equipoise.

Meaning 18: Since Natural Mind, directionless space, has never rejected anything, delusions and karma, like clouds and mist, arise and dissolve. Whatever is grasped within Pure Awareness never passes outside of Natural Mind. All of existence appears and is released within Natural Mind. Since positive and negative are undifferentiated, there is no dividing of Natural Mind. Since it is never clarified or obscured, it is wide open day and night.

Thus she spoke.

The Gyer Dakini Drag-chen Tsal showed Dakini Namkha Nyima Öden Ma sign number 19: pressing her palms to her waist on each side.

Meaning 19: Since Natural Mind is immeasurable it is primordially size-less. Since Dharmakaya is spontaneously existent, discrimination of good and bad is self-liberated. Since faults are destroyed from the base, good qualities are naturally complete. Since the King of Awareness is realized, delusions are already annihilated.

Thus she spoke.

Dakini Namkha Nyima Öden Ma showed Dakini Nyima Tong-Kyab Ma sign number 20: the sign of a heart, like three magical mirrors.

Meaning 20: Since space is unrestricted, don't tether it with dualistic grasping. If you cannot be unreactive to dualistic appearances, the sun of wisdom will set. If thought does not arise as Natural Mind, you will try to climb the paths and stages but wisdom will disappear. If you do not befriend the demon of negative emotions your path of practice will become impossible.

Thus she spoke.

Dakini Nyima Tong-Kyab Ma showed Dakini Maha Sukasiddhi sign number 21: the sign of Pure Awareness's own radiance;

pressing down on the body.

Meaning 21: If you don't hold the meaning with confidence, the daughter of effort will run wild. If you don't accept protection from the guardian of the view, the dear one, your own mind, will be destroyed like an enemy. If you don't post the sentry of meditation, being known as a great yogi will be meaningless. If you don't tame the wild elephant of conduct, your view will become that of an ordinary person.

Thus she spoke.

The Dakini Maha Sukasiddhi showed the Cho family Dakini Bon-chig sign number 22: the sign of clear meaning, hands joined.

Meaning 22: Since Natural Mind has no past or future, it is connected to all Buddhas of the three times. Since Natural Mind includes immeasurable compassion, it is connected to all sentient beings. Realizing it is the place of all arising, abiding, and dissolving; it is connected with all paths and results. Since emptiness and appearances are liberated in Pure Awareness, the fruit is attained without effort.

Thus she spoke.

The Cho family Dakini Bon-chig showed sign number 23: collecting the life-essence of the Gurus.

Meaning 23: Since it is not born from causes and conditions, there is no basis for an original production. Since it abides in the great unknown, in the middle there is no place of abiding. Since Dharmakaya is immutable, there is no way for it to end. Since existence is liberated in the ultimate sphere of Pure Awareness there are no resultant three Bodies that were sought to be attained.

Thus she spoke.

Sign number 24 is the White AH Mind Transference.

Meaning 24: In Self-Originated Wisdom there is no reliance upon paths and stages to be attained. Since it does not rely upon cause and effect, it is a radiance that pervades space. It is not interrupted by conditions, nor destroyed by antidotes. Since Pure Awareness is self-liberated, the result is free of production and destruction.

Thus she spoke.

Sign number 25 is Guru Yoga at the crown.

Meaning 25: This self-originated Wisdom Awareness has never been produced or destroyed by causes and conditions. There is no enumeration of paths, stages, and results. It is free of being an object of the seventeen concepts.

Thus she spoke.

Sign number 26 is six self-clear, turning wheels.

Meaning 26: Since a thunderbolt of awareness arises from emptiness, causes of attainment are self-liberated. Since a thunderbolt of awareness transcending cause and effect arises, sequential paths (yana-vehicles) are self-liberated. Since a thunderbolt of awareness transcending the faulty arises, grasping is self-liberated. Since a thunderbolt of awareness of emptiness and appearances arises, a fabricator is self-liberated.

Thus she spoke.

Sign number 27 is pointing out Natural Mind with an illuminating mirror.

Meaning 27: Natural Mind is unborn, beyond the way of words, whether simply or elaborately spoken; and beyond the four dualistic conventionalities: existing, seeing, appearing, or being conventionally accepted reality. This is the perspective of Dzogchen.

Thus she spoke.

Sign number 28 is offering the body in a feast-gathering (tsog-ganacakra).

Meaning 28: Self-liberated, Natural Mind is the essence of the meaning of Emptiness. Views asserting singularity (partisanship) or multiplicity are a pitfall. Beyond all hope and fear, beyond effort, Natural Mind is a vast vessel of great bliss.

Thus she spoke.

Sign number 29 is the mudra of the lion released.

Meaning 29: Because Awareness is completely pure, even the name samsara does not exist. Without abandoning the five aggregates, enlightenment is primordially attained. All the ornaments illuminating Natural Mind are complete. Samantabhadra equanimity does not fall into partisanship.

Thus she spoke.

Sign number 30 is the sign of being shielded by the Lord's command.

Meaning 30: Those who don't abide in this, who lack the fortune for it, are like someone who wants yogurt trying to milk a horn, or a dog trying to lick at space. This is a place of raksha-cannibals where the brightness of the elements has faded. By mixing nectar with poison you cut short the lives of living beings. By mixing-up view, meditation, conduct, and fruition you enter a pit of darkness. Degeneration of samaya will make heart's-blood pour from your mouth.

Thus she spoke.

SAMAYAPATA

The End

I am the learned Drenpa Namkha.

This Female Lineage that grants relief was written with lapis ink on copper sheets.

These signs of the lineage were transmitted by a succession of Mahasiddha Dakinis.

For fortunate beings to attain Liberation, it was entrusted to disciples of future generations.

Foolish kings and ministers changed Bön into Dharma. The lamp of Bön teachings was hidden underground.

This mind-transmission, which is like gold, Was not hidden underground but kept in my mind.

It has been transmitted heart to heart by fortunate ones. It is the essence of the teachings, not common to everyone.

If you do not keep it from those with degenerate samaya, your life will be shortened.

Thus he said.

sealed-sealed-sealed
sealed-sealed-sealed
sealed-sealed-sealed
It is sealed with nine seals.

This 'Thirty Signs of the Female Lineage' Is the heart-drop of Je Ritröpa.

It was passed to Tulku Lung-tön Lha-nyen. He transmitted it to Lung-gom Korlo Gyalpo.

E THI

Additional Meditation

Relax your body and mind. Let go and release your mind without any movement. Just as if you have knots tied in a rope, untie them; these knots are any grasping. Relax without any thought of containing or stopping thoughts.

If a thought arises, do not concern yourself with it. It is as if whatever clouds develop, they dissolve into space. So stay in this continuity, the appearance-manifesting awareness. Within experience, the emptiness factor or the appearance factor may be more apparent. It makes no difference.

This is what we do. This is the way we meditate: quietly. Even if disturbing thoughts or appearances arise, we will be able to sustain the meditation. We want to be able to bring this awareness back to mind during the course of our life, whether we are driving down the road, working, cooking, or with any activity. Eventually, you will be able to sustain your awareness all the time.

It doesn't matter what is arising in your mind, whether good or bad. We just look at it and settle in the Natural State. Sit comfortably in the usual meditation posture. As it is said, "meditate, meditate, don't meditate. Settle, settle, don't settle. Settle without settling." It is also said, "Wander, wander, don't wander." This attention to whatever is arising brings us into the Natural State. Ultimately we need non-distraction, so we settle into non-distraction. This is what we call meditation. There is no meditation that is beyond or superior to this. No further explanation is necessary.

Guru Yoga - Khandro Choza Bonmo

Visualize the seated Golden Goddess at a size that's comfortable for you in the space before you. Visualize light rays emanating from her heart and striking us, first of all in the nature of wisdom fire, which burns away all obscurations in our mind, all karmic traces, and especially any hindrances to our understanding of the teachings. Then, the nature of wisdom water comes to wash away the same. Then a third time, light rays in the nature of wisdom wind comes to blow away all those obscurations and hindrances to our realizing the instructions. From the crown of the Great Mother Sphere comes a white Ah which dissolves into our crown, endowing us with all the qualities of enlightened body; from her throat comes a red Om which dissolves into our throat, endowing us with all the qualities of enlightened speech; and, from her heart comes a blue Hung which dissolves into our heart, endowing us with all the qualities of enlightened mind. By that, we come to be endowed with all the qualities of enlightened body, speech and mind of Buddhahood.

Now let us meditate just as we did before. We are really focusing on the Bonku, the Dharmakaya, within ourselves. Relax body and mind. Keep the spine erect. This is to keep the flow of energy in the channels and to keep the energy that flows within the channels balanced. Then the mind will be relaxed. This helps us to rest in the Natural Mind.

As you rest in the Natural Mind, undoubtedly thoughts will arise. But do not take any special interest in them. Do not pay attention to their content. Do not follow after them, and do not stop them. Just leave your mind completely relaxed. Let all holding or clinging dissolve. Do not pay attention to any object whatsoever. You may gain an experience, a meditative equipoise, like space. If that kind of experience arises, rest in it. Like when we look at things with our eyes, the clear light dawns within us. Continuously remain in that experience without contriving anything or altering anything. Just continuously rest within the inseparability of emptiness and illumination. Do not think "Oh, it's empty" or "it's luminous." Cultivate the experience and stay in its continuity. If a thought arises and the mind follows after it, just recognize that it happened. Then bring yourself back to the previous absorption.

Note: Everyday, when you have time, meditate.

One of Master Drenpa Namkha's disciples asked him, "Please give me only one sentence to attain enlightenment." Drenpa Namkha responded, "All phenomena are baseless. Realize that, and you will attain enlightenment." Understand and focus on that. This is the meditation that we are doing here. If you recognize the Natural Mind, focus on it, meditate on it, then there is nothing that is not included in that. Your entire world is included within that. It would seem that there is only one earth, one world, but actually the world is individual to each of us. That world exists in relation to us individually. There are actually that many worlds. When we are born, the world that we experience comes into existence. And when we die, that world of our existence disappears. The general world does not disintegrate or disappear. This is the meaning of "all appearances and existence arise out of the Natural Mind, abide in the Natural Mind and dissolve back into the Natural Mind." The Natural Mind is what we call the Great Mother Sphere. This lineage of the Dakini Dzogchen teachings is very much related to this subject. All phenomena arise, abide and dissolve within the Great Mother. All these Dakinis that we are talking about have already attained enlightenment on this basis.

About the Geshe Dangsong Namgyal

Geshe Dangsong Namgyal is a Yungdrung Bön and Rimé Dzogchen teacher primarily giving instructions on Natural Mind meditation. He entered the monastery in Tibet at a young age, eventually leaving Tibet to seek more in-depth teachings. After 25 years studying and teaching at Menri and Sera Je monasteries in India and Tritsen Norbutse Monastery in Nepal, he now teaches in the United States and online.

As a researcher of ancient Tibetan history, culture and religion, he has presented at numerous conferences and seminars around the world, has written many books in Tibetan, and is translating and introducing ancient wisdom teachings previously not presented to Westerners. He published his first English book, *Pure Dzogchen: Zhang Zhung Tradition,* in 2018.

Acknowledgments

I would like to express my deepest appreciation to the great Dzogchen yogi Lama Rinchen Lodo and Lopon Dangsong Lodo who researched ancient texts for the Dakini signs and mudras in preparation for the sacred drawings which have been created by Norbu Lhundrub.

Gratitude for all those who translated, transcribed, reviewed, edited and contributed their efforts in the production of this book. In particular, I would like to express heartfelt gratitude to translator David Molk and all of my dharma students, especially Hal Blacker, Gale Petti, Kate Hitt, and Antoinette Bauer-Smedberg.

I would also like to express my appreciation to the Kunsang Gar Board members and sangha for their continuing support and participation in many great Dharma activities, out of which this book has come to fruition.

www.ingramcontent.com/pod-product-compliance
Lightning Source LLC
Chambersburg PA
CBHW020829020526
44118CB00032B/407